To:

....

From:

....

ONE
DEVOTION
A DAY
FOR
BOYS
N
E
W
S

Daily Wisdom and
Encouragement

Print ISBN 979-8-89151-133-0

Published by Barbour Publishing, Inc., 1810 Barbour Drive, Uhrichsville, Ohio 44683, www.barbourbooks.com

Our mission is to inspire the world with the life-changing message of the Bible.

Printed in China.
002512 0625 HA

DAILY DEVOTIONS FOR BRAVE BOYS

"Be strong and have strength of heart."
DEUTERONOMY 31:6

Bravery might be jumping into a river to save someone who's drowning. Or it might be standing up for a classmate who's being bullied. Or it might be staying true to God and His Word when nobody else seems to care.

Are those things easy? No. But if you love God—if you follow His Son, Jesus—you can be brave in every situation. Why? Because God will give you *His own power* to stand up for the truth, to show love to all, even to do dangerous physical things. He'll give you the courage you need to pursue big dreams—the dreams He gives you—to become a strong man of God who looks out for others.

This book contains 365 devotions, one for every day of the year. Each reading highlights what God's Word says to brave boys. Even if you don't feel brave, keep reading—the Bible has the power to give you strength. Whether you're dealing with fears, choices, family, forgiveness, the future, or any other challenge of life, these devotions will show you what God's Word has to say. . .and build the foundation for a life of bravery.

THE BOOK OF LIFE

All the Holy Writings are God-given and are made alive by Him. Man is helped when he is taught God's Word. It shows what is wrong. It changes the way of a man's life. It shows him how to be right with God.
2 Timothy 3:16

There are lots of helpful books. Some will teach you to throw a curveball, start a business, or grill the perfect hamburger. But only one book can show you "how to be right with God."

Yep, it's the Bible. Whatever you call it—"scripture," "God's Word," or "the Holy Writings"—that big old book is absolutely necessary for life. Why? Because, as today's verse says, it shows us what is wrong (our sin) and how to be right with God (by believing in the death and resurrection of Jesus Christ). If we let it, the Bible will truly change our way of life. It will make us kinder, more generous, wiser, more honest, gentler, more caring, and braver.

The Bible is truly the book of life. Why not spend some time with it now?

Father God, I want to know You through Your Word. Please speak to me as I read.

FOLLOWER'S CHOICE

"If you think it is wrong to serve the Lord, choose today whom you will serve. Choose the gods your fathers worshiped on the other side of the river, or choose the gods of the Amorites in whose land you are living. But as for me and my family, we will serve the Lord."
JOSHUA 24:15

Maybe you've eaten at a buffet restaurant where you can choose from all kinds of food, whatever type you want. If you want pizza, burgers, or salad, they have it. Some people think that what they believe about God is like that kind of restaurant. They choose what they want to believe and leave the rest for someone else.

When God called Joshua, he had to choose whether or not he would follow. Joshua did choose God, and then he told everyone around him about that decision.

God wants *you* to choose too. Will you follow Him? He doesn't want you to mix other beliefs with His Word. He wants you to serve Him, and Him alone.

That's the best choice ever.

Father, I don't want to pick and choose what I believe. I want to follow You alone.

THE LORD'S PLAN

There are many plans in a man's heart,
but it is the Lord's plan that will stand.
PROVERBS 19:21

You may have heard the saying "If you want to make God laugh, tell Him your plans." Even some non-Christians say it. They realize that something beyond themselves controls their lives. Christians don't have to wonder what that "something" is—we know it's God.

In the Old Testament, seventeen-year-old Joseph was sold into slavery by his own brothers. He was carried off to Egypt, where he was jailed on false charges. But God was with Joseph, and in time he became the second most powerful man in the country. Years later, a famine drove Joseph's brothers to Egypt, and they ended up at his door. When Joseph told them who he really was, they were scared.

"You planned to do a bad thing to me," Joseph said, after urging them not to be afraid. "But God planned it for good, to make it happen that many people should be kept alive" (Genesis 50:20).

When you go through things you don't understand—and don't like—be encouraged. The Lord's plan will stand.

Lord, help me trust Your plan for my life.

DAY 4

MISUNDERSTOOD KINDNESS

Love is kind. Love is not jealous. Love does not put itself up as being important. Love has no pride.
1 CORINTHIANS 13:4

What do most boys want to be known for? Being smart? Being strong? Being cool? How about being kind?

For many guys, kindness isn't at the top of the list. People who are kind are sometimes thought of as weak or uncool or even simpleminded. But kindness is often misunderstood.

It's easy to be mean to someone who is different from you—but kindness requires strength. Being kind when others aren't might seem like an uncool choice, but Jesus doesn't care what other people think about you. He cares what *you* think about *Him* and wants you to show His love to others, whether that's considered cool or not. Because Jesus commands it, being kind is the smartest choice.

Are you brave enough, strong enough, and smart enough to choose kindness? Even if you honestly answer no, God is kind enough to give you the help you need. Just ask!

Lord, please give me the courage, strength, and wisdom I need to be kind today—especially when people around me are being mean.

POWER UP

"But you will receive power when the Holy Spirit comes into your life. You will tell about Me in the city of Jerusalem and over all the countries of Judea and Samaria and to the ends of the earth."

Acts 1:8

If you like superhero stories, you probably know how many of them got their superpowers. The Green Lantern has a special ring, Spider-Man was bitten by a radioactive bug, and the Hulk was exposed to gamma radiation.

When we accept Jesus as our Savior, He gives us the gift of eternal life. But He also gives us the power of the Holy Spirit. The Spirit then gives us all the power we need to do Jesus' work on earth. When we follow the Holy Spirit's leading, we become God's champions by spreading His gift of salvation through Jesus.

It might be scary to tell another person about Jesus. You don't know if they'll be excited or maybe make fun of you. The good news is that when we do God's work, *He* provides the help we need—through the powerful gift of the Holy Spirit!

Father, teach me to listen to Your Spirit as I live each day.

WITH ALL YOUR HEART

"This day the Lord your God tells you to obey these Laws. Be careful to obey them with all your heart and with all your soul."
DEUTERONOMY 26:16

Why is it so important to obey God? Because He knows what's best for you. And reading your Bible will help you know what He wants you to do.

In the Bible, there are tons of stories in which God told people what to do. When they were obedient, their lives were blessed. For example, the disciples obeyed Jesus and He provided for all their needs. The very first disciples were fishermen, and when Jesus met them, He told them to leave their jobs behind and follow Him instead. Do you think you could do that?

Well, those first four guys—Peter and Andrew, James and John—didn't wait around and wonder. They did exactly what Jesus asked, and they lived and worked with Him for three years.

Obey God's words with all your heart. Don't worry. . .He'll take care of you!

Lord God, please help me to follow Your plan for my life. May I obey quickly and completely.

IT'S YOUR TURN

"I am your Teacher and Lord. I have washed your feet. You should wash each other's feet also."
John 13:14

Here's a mystery for you: Why, when God's Son, Jesus Christ, came to earth, did *He* do the dirty work?

Feet can be pretty gross. They often smell gross too. It's bad enough to wash your own dirty feet (you *do* wash your feet, right?). It's *super* bad to have to wash anyone else's dirty feet. So why would Jesus stoop so low? Remember, He's God's Son! Everyone else should have been washing *His* feet, right?

Yet look again at today's Bible verse. Jesus served His disciples. Then His disciples served others. Those people served still others, and that cycle continued up until today. Now it's *your* turn.

Oh, maybe not to wash someone's feet. But there are hundreds of other good things you can do for the people nearby. You don't have to wait until you're a grown-up—God can use you right now. That's very good news, indeed!

Lord, wow—You want to use me today to serve other people. Help me to do a great job!

THE GIFT OF A PRAYER

"Give my son Solomon a perfect heart to keep Your Words and Your Laws and to obey them all."
1 Chronicles 29:19

Most dads want the best for their children. They might want their sons to follow in their footsteps and do the same kind of work they do. They might encourage their children to go to college. They might want their children to play sports or write books or make music.

When King David thought of his son Solomon, he had a different idea about what was best. David chose Solomon from all his sons to be the next king of Israel. David didn't ask God to give Solomon great strength. His request wasn't for fame or money for his son. David wanted Solomon to guard God's words, know His laws, and obey His commands.

God answered David's prayer. Solomon became the wisest king on earth!

You can have God's best too. Pray David's prayer for yourself now—and someday you might pray it for your own children.

Father, give me a perfect heart to keep Your words and Your laws and to obey them all.

LOVING THE CHURCH

I am a friend to all who fear You and of those who keep Your Law.
Psalm 119:63

Christians are called to love their fellow Christians more deeply than other people. Jesus once taught, "You are to love each other. You must love each other as I have loved you. If you love each other, all men will know you are My followers" (John 13:34–35). And Jesus' best friend, John, wrote, "We know we have passed from death into life. We know this because we love the Christians" (1 John 3:14).

In today's verse, the psalm writer calls himself a friend of fellow believers. True friends care more about the other person than themselves. They listen to, pray for, and help out their friends in any way possible. And as they do, the "body of Christ"—every believer, everywhere—gets stronger and healthier.

Of course, you should still have friends who aren't believers so you can show them how to follow Jesus. But you should feel a much deeper connection with your Christian friends.

Brave boys are friends to all who keep God's law.

Father, help me to love the people in Your church well.

DAY 10

GOD ALWAYS FORGIVES YOU

Praise the Lord, O my soul. And forget none of His acts of kindness. He forgives all my sins.
Psalm 103:2–3

Evan and his dad were sitting on the edge of the boy's bed. Both of them were mad. Evan blurted out, "You're the worst dad in the world!"

Evan's dad was quiet for a while. Then he asked, "Evan, what you've just said—is that true, or is that just how you feel?" It's amazing what a calming effect a question like this has during a moment of heated emotions.

"It's just how I feel," Evan admitted. His dad's shoulders relaxed. Evan's shoulders relaxed too. He realized what he had said wasn't true. Evan and his dad forgave each other.

God, our Father in heaven, never sins against us, so we never need to forgive Him. But how good to know that "He forgives all my sins." All you have to do is ask!

Lord, I thank You that You always forgive me when I say or do something bad. Please help me to forgive others when they upset me.

YOUR GIFT

Be sure to use the gift God gave you.
1 Timothy 4:14

There's a famous saying that goes, "Your talent is God's gift to you. What you do with it is your gift back to God."

That means that God has given each of us some special ability, and it would make God happy if we used it! Some guys are good at playing the guitar, some guys are talented at starting businesses, and some guys have the interest and capability to become doctors and take care of people's medical needs. Of course, that list goes on and on.

It's okay if you don't know yet what your special talent is. But once you've figured it out, use it to make God happy. Whether it's leading worship at your church, serving as a firefighter, or working as a school janitor, do the best job you can. When you do, you honor the God who made you. You make His world a better place. . .and you might just point other people to Him.

That's using the gift God gave you!

Father, help me to know what my talents are and to use them to make You happy.

DAY 12

STRONGER AND STRONGER

"The one who is right with God will hold to his way. And he who has clean hands will become stronger and stronger."
Job 17:9

Did you know the devil once made a bet with God? Satan saw a very good man named Job and thought he only served God in order to get good things. Satan thought he could turn Job away from God, and the Lord basically said, *Okay, try*.

So Satan got to work, attacking everything that was important to Job. The devil took away Job's money, his ten children, even his health. One day things were going great for Job, and the next day life was awful.

Job was sad, no doubt about it. But instead of quitting, he handed his pain over to God. Job never stopped trusting that God would hear his prayers—even some very unhappy prayers.

At one point, Job even said that people who trust God get stronger and stronger. Whatever hard thing you're going through, be like Job. Keep praying, and trust that God will always be with you.

Lord, there are days when nothing seems to go my way. Remind me that You are always with me.

DAY 13

WHAT SHOULD I PRAY?

You must pray at all times as the Holy Spirit leads you to pray. Pray for the things that are needed. You must watch and keep on praying. Remember to pray for all Christians.
EPHESIANS 6:18

Many verses in the Bible tell us to pray. Some, like Ephesians 6:18, even tell us to pray "at all times." There are all kinds of things we *could* pray for, but have you ever wondered if there are certain things that we *should* pray for?

Jesus told us just what to pray for in His famous "Sermon on the Mount." Here's what He said: "Pray like this: 'Our Father in heaven, Your name is holy. May Your holy nation [or kingdom] come. What you want done, may it be done on earth as it is in heaven. Give us the bread we need today. Forgive us our sins as we forgive those who sin against us. Do not let us be tempted, but keep us from sin'" (Matthew 6:9–13).

If you are looking for the perfect prayer to pray anytime, this is it.

Lord Jesus, I thank You for making prayer so easy to understand!

DAY 14

DON'T BE AFRAID

When he saw the angel, Zacharias was troubled and afraid.
LUKE 1:12

Have you ever had a dream that made you wake up in fear? Then you probably know how Zacharias felt. He had never met an angel before, but suddenly there was one right in front of him—and Zacharias *wasn't* dreaming.

He might have been breathing fast, sweating, or looking for a way out. Zacharias was too scared to think straight, too frightened to listen well—even though the angel had good news to share.

You've been scared at times, haven't you? We all have. But no matter how frightened we are, God is always with us. And He doesn't want us to live our lives in fear.

We can't just stop being afraid on our own. We will need help, just like Zacharias did. The angel told him, "Do not be afraid," and explained that God had heard his prayers for a son. Even better, God was going to answer them!

There's no trouble God can't handle, and nothing scares Him. Why should anything scare us?

Lord, I have been scared and didn't even ask You for help. Next time, make me remember You.

BIG DREAMS

The king said to me, "What are you asking for?" So I prayed to the God of heaven. And I said to the king, "If it pleases the king, and if your servant has found favor in your eyes, send me to Judah, to the city of my fathers' graves. Let me build it again."
NEHEMIAH 2:4–5

Throughout history, young men have rushed to serve their country in wartime. Teenagers even pretended they were older so they could join the army and fight. This love of country is called "patriotism."

In the Bible, Nehemiah loved his nation of Judah. But it was destroyed in war because the people turned away from God. The nation of Persia now ruled over Judah, and Nehemiah—who worked for the Persian king—dreamed of going home to rebuild the wrecked city of Jerusalem.

This was no selfish dream. Nehemiah wanted to honor God and point the people back to Him. God approved Nehemiah's dream and caused Persia to let him rebuild Jerusalem.

Big dreams come from our big God. If He gives you a desire to serve, He'll also provide the opportunity.

Lord, please use me for big things—Your dreams!

DAY 16

NO ONE IN NEED

No one was in need. All who owned houses or pieces of land sold them and brought the money from what was sold. They gave it to the missionaries. It was divided to each one as he had need.

Acts 4:34–35

An eighth grader in Louisiana saw some classmates in need and decided to do something. Chase Neyland-Square set up a closet at his school, then filled it with clothes and supplies for any student who needed them.

"I know that everybody doesn't have things, and I'm fortunate to have things that other people don't have," Chase told a TV reporter from Baton Rouge. "How would I feel in that situation?"

This boy's goal was for nobody in his school to be in need. This was the goal of the early Christians too. They sold their things and divided up the money to help each other. Few people in our world live that way—but brave boys think as much of others as they think of themselves. Could you do something like Chase did? Find a need, and then do what you can to meet it.

God, show me how to live like the early Christians.

DAY 17

LEARN, TRUST, SHARE

So then, faith comes to us by hearing the Good News. And the Good News comes by someone preaching it.
ROMANS 10:17

How do you learn things? If you're at school, you listen to the teacher in the front of the classroom. Some people watch online tutorials. Many people learn by reading books.

Whatever the method, the learning *process* is basically the same. First, someone has to share information with you. Second, you trust that what you've learned is true and make it part of your life. Third, when you have learned something good, you probably want to share it.

Faith works the same way. Someone helped you realize that you are a sinner in need of a Savior. They told you about Jesus and His sacrifice on the cross so you could be right with God. You trusted Jesus for salvation. Now you should want to share it with others.

God's love is for everyone, but not everyone has heard the message yet. Who will you share the good news with today?

Lord, please give me courage to share the good news of Your love with someone today.

DAY 18

TROUBLE AND HOPE

"I have told you these things so you may have peace in Me. In the world you will have much trouble. But take hope! I have power over the world!"
JOHN 16:33

Have you noticed how honest the Bible is? It tells how even the biggest heroes made mistakes. It says that even if you follow God, you'll have trouble in this world. In fact, the Bible *promises* trouble for Christians!

Jesus knew trouble awaited His twelve disciples—and every other person (like you) who would follow Him in the future. So He said honestly, "The time will come when anyone who kills you will think he is helping God" (John 16:2). Yikes! But then He spoke the words of the verse above. Yes, you'll have "much trouble" in this world. "But take hope!" Jesus said. "I have power over the world!"

That power makes Christians brave. Whether you're facing death for Jesus or just being teased at school, He is stronger. No matter what happens on earth, He has rewards in heaven that we can't even imagine. He tells us these things so we can have peace.

I praise You, Jesus, for Your power over the world.

FROM FEAR TO COURAGE

God cannot lie. We who have turned to Him can have great comfort knowing that He will do what He has promised.
Hebrews 6:18

Moses and Joshua had the courage to obey God because they wholeheartedly believed His promises. In turn, they coached God's people to take courage.

Sadly, the people of Israel often gave in to fear and disobeyed God. If you find yourself filled with fear, you may have forgotten who God is. It's also likely that you have forgotten what God has promised.

Like Moses and Joshua, you can draw on your sources of courage. But they're not your own physical strength and brain power. Instead, as Moses and Joshua proved, they are the *presence* and the *promises* of the Lord God.

How good that you can be filled with courage every day! You can have courage in every situation because of the Lord's promises and His constant presence in your life.

Lord, I want to trade fear for courage. Help me to remember that You are always with me. And help me to remember Your wonderful promises.

NO ONE LEFT OUT

"This is what I tell you to do:
Love each other just as I have loved you."
JOHN 15:12

Everyone wants to be treated with respect. But too often people treat each other like bothers rather than blessings. Have you ever been treated badly? Have you ever treated someone else badly?

Jesus said He wanted the people who love Him to love other people. Why? Because He's all about love.

Jesus loved you first, even when you were at your worst. So He doesn't give you a pass on loving anyone else. Love the people who irritate you—that even means enemies. It means loving those people who no one talks to, those people who get picked on, and those people who pick on others—even if they pick on *you*.

Jesus loves you. He expects you to love others. Don't be surprised if people think that's strange. You might say obeying Jesus is brave!

Father, since I accept Your love, I need to share Your love. Since You didn't leave anyone out of Your plan to love, neither should I.

DAY 21

FOLLOW JESUS CHRIST'S EXAMPLE

These things are all a part of the Christian life to which you have been called. Christ suffered for us. This shows us we are to follow in His steps.
1 Peter 2:21

By the time He was twelve or thirteen years old, Jesus worked alongside His earthly father, Joseph, who was a carpenter. Back in Bible times, carpenters didn't just work with wood—they also made things with bricks, stone, and other building materials. The work was hard, and the days were long.

Those years were a piece of cake, though, compared to the day Jesus was whipped and then nailed to a rough Roman cross.

Jesus is God's Son, always and forever the king of the universe. But He was willing to live thirty-three years here on earth. What's more, He was willing to *die* for the sins of the whole world. His terrible death and glorious resurrection made a way for people to be adopted into God's family.

Jesus paid the ultimate price to give you the ultimate gift. In turn, you have the opportunity of a lifetime: trusting and obeying Him.

Lord, You ask me to live for You. I will!

BE READY!

"You must be ready also. The Son of Man is coming at a time when you do not think He will come."
MATTHEW 24:44

Jesus had hiked up the Mount of Olives. When He sat down, His followers asked Him when the end of world would come. (People are still curious about that!) But rather than answering the question directly, Jesus gave the disciples something better—He told them how to be prepared for His return.

Jesus warned His followers that many people would claim to *be* Him—but those people would just be lying. He told the disciples that they would hear about wars, food shortages, earthquakes, persecution, false teachers, you name it. But that was just the beginning of the end.

Then Jesus shared a secret: He will return when most people don't think He's going to. That means we always need to be ready to meet Him.

How can you be ready? Well, don't ever do anything you'd be embarrassed by if Jesus were to suddenly appear. Instead, bravely do what the Bible tells you to do, every minute of every day.

Lord Jesus, by Your grace,
I want to be ready for Your return.

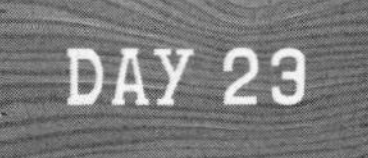

DON'T JUST TALK ABOUT IT

My children, let us not love with words or in talk only. Let us love by what we do and in truth.
1 John 3:18

Perhaps you've heard of "good intentions." That means you *think* about helping someone out, and you might even *talk* about it—but you never actually *do* anything. Does that really help anyone?

One of Jesus' brothers, James, wrote this: "What if a Christian does not have clothes or food? And one of you says to him, 'Goodbye, keep yourself warm and eat well.' But if you do not give him what he needs, how does that help him? A faith that does not do things is a dead faith" (James 2:15–17).

It's the combination of words and actions that proves we love people. And that's exactly what Jesus wants from us. Yes, let's tell people we care. But don't just talk about it. *Do* good things!

Lord God, please help me to truly love people. May I prove my love by my words and my actions.

STAY CLOSE

"But man is born to trouble, as fire goes up."
Job 5:7

Job was a man in the Bible who went through some incredibly hard times. For a while, trouble followed him everywhere. Job loved God, so why was his life so tough? Because the devil thought Job would stop trusting God if life got too hard. With God's permission, as a test, Satan took away Job's children and everything else that was important to him.

No surprise here—Job was sad. He told his friend that his burdens were like an army lined up against him, and that they were too much to bear. But through all of the struggles, Job never turned away from God.

Everyone has bad days. Some are worse than others, and some seem impossible. But God wants you to know that He will work everything out for you. The devil wants you to be sad and discouraged, to stop relying on God. But you know better. Be like Job, and stay close to God.

Lord, some days life is tough. I don't understand why I have to go through all the troubles. Help me to remember that You love me!

WAIT FOR IT. . .

"I wait for Your saving power, O Lord."
GENESIS 49:18

Sometimes waiting is really hard. Do you like waiting for Christmas morning? How about the last day of school? Or your family's vacation to the beach? All of us struggle to wait for exciting things.

But patience is very important. For one thing, you can't make time go any faster, so impatience will just make you miserable. And if you try to rush ahead of *God's* timing for something, you can really mess up your life.

Kids often want to go places, see things, and have stuff that they really aren't ready for. That's why God tells parents to train and protect their kids. If they say no and you get frustrated (and it happens to everyone), step back and take a deep breath. Don't try to be too grown up, too fast. . .trust your parents to know what's best for you and when.

In a way, that's God's "saving power" in your life. Wait for it—someday you'll be glad you did.

Heavenly Father, please help me to be patient in good times and especially in the difficult ones.

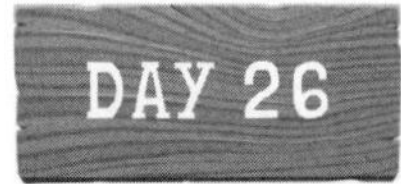

NO-WORRY BIRDS

"Look at the birds. They do not plant seeds. They do not gather grain. They have no grain buildings for keeping grain. Yet God feeds them. Are you not worth more than the birds?"
LUKE 12:24

Imagine a flock of "farming fowl"—birds that hoe the ground, plant seeds, and operate bird-sized tractors to harvest their grain. Would they wear overalls? Would they go to farm shows to learn all the latest research? Would they worry over the weather forecast?

Actually, birds just fly from one meal to the next, finding food pretty much wherever they turn. They leave the farming to someone else. Who is that? Well, God!

And you know what God said about the birds? That you're worth more than they are. If God said it, you know it's true. And if He takes care of those birds—billions and billions of them all over the world—then He can take care of You. In fact, He's done that every day of your life.

So, what are you worried about? If God's handling everything, there are better ways to spend your time—like telling Him "thanks."

Father, please help me to be grateful rather than anxious.

DAY 27

GOD'S MESSAGE

No part of the Holy Writings came long ago because of what man wanted to write. But holy men who belonged to God spoke what the Holy Spirit told them.
2 Peter 1:21

The Bible is more than just a book—it's really a collection of books. It's like sixty-six books all glued together under one cover.

Did you know that around forty people wrote the Bible? The authors include familiar names like Moses, Daniel, Isaiah, Matthew, and Paul—and some less famous guys like Obadiah and Habakkuk. They wrote from different times and places, but they each had one very important thing in common: God's Holy Spirit told them what to say.

It's true! When you read the Bible, you're reading exactly what God wants you to know. The Bible isn't just the ideas of men—it's the perfect, powerful truth of God. It's the life-changing invitation that welcomes us into God's family. It's the wise and good and hopeful message that lets us live with courage in a crazy world.

The Bible is God's message to people—to *you*. Make sure you know what it says.

Lord, please help me to read and understand Your Word.

A GLAD HEART

A glad heart is good medicine,
but a broken spirit dries up the bones.
Proverbs 17:22

There are things in life that make us sad: Someone you love is dying. A parent's job is going poorly. Some kids at school are making fun of you.

But sometimes you're sad without any particular reason. You can't put your finger on why, you just aren't happy. And it doesn't help if someone says, "Cheer up!"

Since it's part of God's Word, Proverbs 17:22 is absolutely true. But how can we get from those sad times to the place where we have the "good medicine" of a "glad heart"?

It will be a process. And it will probably take time. First step, pray. Tell God that you're sad, and ask Him to heal your broken spirit. Next step, read His Word. Look for promises like Psalm 28:7 or Philippians 4:4. Finally, look for people and messages that remind you of God's goodness and love. Stay away from sad movies, angry music, and complaining people.

Over time, you may find that you're feeling happier again. That "heart medicine" works!

Lord God, please help me to live a joyful Christian life.

OTHER PEOPLE'S NEEDS

Do not work only for your own good.
Think of what you can do for others.
1 Corinthians 10:24

It is easy to be selfish. We human beings are hardwired to take care of our own needs first. When you are hungry, your belly rumbles. When you are thirsty, your throat gets dry. You know when to get food and water for yourself because you know those needs personally.

When other people are hungry or thirsty, you don't feel it in the same way. But God tells you to think about others and see their needs too. When you notice that someone has a need, do something about it. Give them some food or water. Listen to them if they need to talk. Hang out with them if they need a friend.

It's natural to take care of yourself. But when you take care of others, you are letting God's love work through you.

Lord, cause me to think about other people more than myself. Give me the love that You have for them and help me to take care of their needs.

DAY 30

KEEP YOUR EYES ON JESUS

Trust in the Lord, and do good.
PSALM 37:3

In this life, you meet people who are not interested in doing the right thing. Don't let them encourage you to do wrong. The Bible says people who always make bad choices wither like dry grass. Instead, God tells you to trust Him and do good things for people. Look for ways you can serve others. That's what Jesus did—and who doesn't want to become more like Him?

Spend time daily with the Lord in His Word and prayer. God will give you everything you need. Decide to live your life for Him, and then trust Him to do what He says He'll do. He will always take care of you.

There will be times when life doesn't seem to make sense. You'll begin to wonder about God's plans. But never forget that He is good all the time. Keep on trusting. Don't worry about what other people have; don't worry about what other people do. Keep your eyes on Jesus!

Lord, help me to trust You no matter what I'm going through. I want You to be proud of me. Thanks for everything You do!

DAY 31

RECEIVE JESUS!

"First of all, look for the holy nation of God. Be right with Him. All these other things will be given to you also."
MATTHEW 6:33

Jesus told people, "My holy nation (or *kingdom*) belongs to children." Not only that, but Jesus said, "Unless you become like a little child, you can't even get into my holy nation."

What was He talking about? Well, what are kids good at doing? They're good at *receiving*. When you're hungry and your mom gives you some food, what do you do? You receive it. God gives you a warm sunny day to go outside and play. . .what do you do? You receive it.

The same idea applies when it comes to God's holy nation. Can you work really hard to be part of Jesus' kingdom? No. Can you pay lots of money to be part of it? No. That's what grown-ups often try to do.

What *do* you have to do to enter God's holy nation? You guessed it: You have to *receive* something. Or, specifically, receive Someone.

Lord Jesus, I gladly receive You. I want to be part of Your holy nation now and forever.

FOLLOW, FAKE IT, OR WALK AWAY

I have chosen the faithful way.
I have set Your Law in front of me.
Psalm 119:30

There are plenty of people who'd like you to follow them. And every day you have a choice. You can follow, fake it, or walk away.

Jesus is one of the people who invites you to follow. The Bible tells what you'll need to do. And you can follow, fake it, or walk away.

When you truly follow Jesus, God calls you faithful. If you fake it, you're not being truthful—and you're not really on God's side. That makes Him sad, as it does if you walk away.

When you study the Bible and learn the things that are important to God, you are never wasting time. When you take what you've learned and live it out, you are showing courage. When you choose the faithful way, God is pleased.

Heavenly Father, I want to honestly follow You. I want to be obedient to Your Word, the Bible. I don't ever want to fake it or walk away.

SPEAK BOLDLY

Paul saw the Lord in a dream one night. He said to Paul, "Do not be afraid. Keep speaking. Do not close your mouth."
ACTS 18:9

Many times, you'll find yourself around people who clearly don't know Jesus. They might be using bad language, or putting other people down, or even insulting God. These people need to hear the truth, but sometimes we're afraid to speak up.

Even the apostle Paul needed courage to speak up. He was one of the founding fathers of the Christian church, as well as the author of many of the letters in the New Testament. But God came to Paul in a dream one night, urging him to keep telling others about Jesus.

When it's scary to talk about Jesus, remember what God told the prophet Isaiah: "I have put My words in your mouth, and have covered you with the shadow of My hand" (Isaiah 51:16). That means we have both God's message and His protection!

When we are obedient, God will fill our mouth with His words. Just ask Him what to say, then open your mouth and speak.

Father, help me to be bold in sharing Your will.

GOD-CONFIDENCE

I will not be afraid of ten thousands of people who stand all around against me.
Psalm 3:6

David wrote Psalm 3 when he was running away from his son Absalom. The guy was a good-looking jerk. He had planned the murder of his own half brother, another one of David's sons, who had hurt Absalom's sister. Before long, Absalom decided that *he* should be king instead of David—and he worked to steal the country away from his dad. He must have done well, because someone reported to David, "The hearts of the men of Israel are with Absalom" (2 Samuel 15:13).

In today's verse, David said tens of thousands of people were against him. To understand how he might have felt, imagine walking onto the 50-yard line of an NFL football field and seeing an entire stadium full of people looking at you. . .none of them friendly.

But David wasn't afraid, because his confidence was in God. "You, O Lord, are a covering around me," he prayed, "my shining-greatness, and the One Who lifts my head" (Psalm 3:3). When you face enemies in life, you can pray the same thing.

Lord, with You, I can face anything.

ALWAYS FORGIVING OTHERS

"If you forgive people their sins,
your Father in heaven will forgive your sins also."
MATTHEW 6:14

Austin couldn't believe it. While he and his friends were playing soccer, he ran over to the sideline for a quick break—and his sports drink was gone. Worse? When Austin looked around, he spotted a little boy chugging it. Ugh!

Then Austin remembered a few things *he* had done as a little boy. So he walked over to the kid, got on his knees, looked him in the eye, and smiled. "You know," Austin said, "it's not good to take someone else's drink, but I forgive you." The little boy didn't say anything. He just looked down and offered to give back the bottle. "No thanks, little guy," Austin said. "You can finish it." Then he ran back onto the field.

When someone does wrong to you—no matter what age they might be—it's always right to forgive. (But next time, you might want to put your sports drink in a hiding place!)

Lord, the next time someone sins against me, I want to do what Austin did—forgive!

DAY 36

BETTER TO OBEY

Samuel said, "Is the Lord pleased as much with burnt gifts as He is when He is obeyed? See, it is better to obey than to give gifts."
1 SAMUEL 15:22

Jesus was brave when He made sure to do everything His Father asked Him to do. To be a brave boy means *you* will work on living each day like Jesus did.

Sometimes it's hard to do what you're told. Imagine you didn't get enough sleep, but your parent is telling you to hurry up and get ready for school. Obeying like Jesus means you act respectfully, getting ready without an attitude.

Remember Adam and Eve? They showed what happens when we *don't* obey. God gave them a beautiful home in Eden, but they disobeyed His one simple rule. Then they had to leave paradise and find a new home that wasn't nearly as nice. Pretty sad, huh?

Whatever the situation, the best gift you can give yourself is to obey God. Yeah, sometimes that's tough—but don't forget that He'll help you do whatever He wants you to do!

Lord, please help me to obey Your commands. I want to live in a way that pleases You.

DAY 37

INVITE OTHERS TO JOIN YOUR TEAM

We should do good to everyone. For sure, we should do good to those who belong to Christ.
GALATIANS 6:10

In the car with his mom one day, ten-year-old Ian saw people standing by street corners holding cardboard signs. Finally, Ian looked at his mom and said, "I wish we could give a peanut butter and jelly sandwich to all of those people." Ian's mom thought that was a great idea. "But how can we make that many sandwiches?" Ian wondered aloud. His mom suggested he invite other people to join his team.

That Sunday, twenty-five friends stayed after church and made 210 PB&J sandwiches. Other people brought hundreds of juice boxes and bags of chips, crates full of apples and oranges, and napkins and paper lunch bags. Everyone had so much fun giving the food away that the team wanted to do it again—and again.

You can't help a lot of people by yourself. But if you invite other people to join your team, you could help hundreds. Wanna give it a try?

Lord, when You ask me to do something big, help me to invite others to join my team.

DAY 38

COURSE CHANGE

He who does not punish his son when he needs it hates him, but he who loves him will punish him when he needs it.
PROVERBS 13:24

If you let a ship drift without someone at the wheel, it won't arrive where you want it to. It might even crash. The same is true of a car. Imagine that you're ready to drive for the first time, but you're sent off without a steering wheel. That's not helpful. In fact, it's dangerous.

The book of Proverbs says that dads love their children best when they make sure they're trained in the way God wants them to go. Just like a wandering ship or car, you can get into trouble if you don't have clear directions. You'll end up sorry if you don't know where to go for directions, why it's important to follow those directions, or how to change directions when you get off course.

So when your dad or mom corrects you, they may not just be criticizing. They probably want the absolute best for you.

Lord, I don't like being corrected, so help me remember it's a way to get me to a better place.

STICK AROUND

A friend loves at all times.
PROVERBS 17:17

Losing friends is never fun, but it happens sometimes.

You've probably lost friends for silly reasons. Maybe they got mad at you because they were jealous about something. Or maybe they heard some gossip about you and believed it—without talking to you first.

God wants you to be a different kind of friend. He wants you to be the kind of guy who sticks around when everyone else is leaving, even when your friend messes up. Especially when he messes up. Why? Because that's the type of friend Jesus is to you.

Sometimes you disobey your parents. Sometimes you think more about yourself than others. And sometimes you tell lies. But Jesus always forgives you when you ask. That's called "grace."

Be a grace-full friend to others. It's a great way to witness to those who don't yet know Jesus. And for those who do know Him, it's a great reminder of the love God shows us through Jesus.

We all make mistakes. Let's all stick around for each other.

Lord, I want to be the type of friend who loves my friends at all times.

EMOTIONS ARE OKAY

Then Jesus cried.
John 11:35

Boys and girls are different—that's just the way God made us. Though our bodies have a lot of similarities, they're not exactly alike. And, in general, the way we think and feel is different too. Girls are usually more emotional than boys.

But that doesn't mean boys can't or shouldn't show emotions. Even Jesus cried after one of His good friends, a man named Lazarus, had died. If Jesus could show that kind of emotion in public, don't you think we can too?

Besides sadness, Jesus expressed emotions like love, anger, compassion, frustration, and everything else people feel. Even though He was God, He was also completely human—and He felt all the same emotions we do. He just kept everything in a perfect balance.

Jesus' example is what we need to aim for. We can get too emotional, whether we're overly angry or we can't stop crying. So we should ask God to help us manage our emotions. He is always glad to make us more like Jesus.

Father, please strengthen me when I'm too weak and soften me when I'm too tough. Make my emotions like those of Jesus.

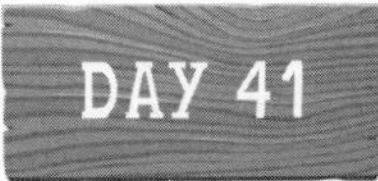

LOVING YOUR NEIGHBOR

You do well when you obey the Holy Writings which say, "You must love your neighbor as you love yourself."
James 2:8

What sets apart your friends from the rest of the people you know? Maybe you and your friends like the same things. Maybe you understand each other well. Whatever it is, it's easier to be nice to your friends because you like them.

But when the Bible says, "You must love your neighbor as you love yourself," it doesn't just mean your friends. It means *everyone*. It even means the people you don't really care for.

God wants Christians to prove they belong to Him by showing love to everyone—especially those people who are hard to love. And that's more than just forcing yourself to say hello to certain people. It means that you treat them the same as if they were one of your good friends.

That's a brave thing to do. But it might just pay off in some surprising new friends!

Lord, help me to treat everyone, not just my friends, with love. Give me the kind of love You have for people who I don't normally get along with.

DAY 42

PAUL AND BARNABAS

Many Jews and others who had become Jews followed Paul and Barnabas as they talked to the Jews. They told them to keep on trusting in the loving-favor of God.
ACTS 13:43

Paul and Barnabas were missionaries, traveling to many cities and telling people how much God loved them. Many people liked and believed their message. But there were some who hated what Paul and Barnabas said. They tried to mess up the missionaries' hard work.

Paul was never afraid to stand up for God. He didn't stop preaching just because some people opposed his message. He just took every chance he had to tell people that Jesus was the Savior, the only one who could save them from their sins. Because Paul and Barnabas didn't quit, God's message went all across the land and many people became believers. They told other people about Jesus, and those people told people. . .and over hundreds and hundreds of years, someone shared that same message with you. How cool is that?

Imagine how God might use *you* to tell others about Jesus. Be brave like Paul and Barnabas.

God, I want to tell people about Your love for them through Jesus.

PRAY INSTEAD

Do not worry. Learn to pray about everything.
Give thanks to God as you ask Him for what you need.
Philippians 4:6

Do you know the story of Chicken Little? One day an acorn falls from a tree, hitting Mr. Little on the head. Surprised, he quickly convinces himself that it was actually the *sky* that struck him. He runs about screaming, "The sky is falling! The sky is falling!"

That's a silly response, right? But we all experience "falling sky" moments at times. It may be at home, at school, or with friends—something happens that makes us want to panic. When you feel fear, stop and pray. Praying can calm you down because you'll remember who is in control of everything—God.

Jesus once said, "Look at the birds in the sky. They do not plant seeds. They do not gather grain. They do not put grain into a building to keep. Yet your Father in heaven feeds them! Are you not more important than the birds?" (Matthew 6:26).

Well, yes you are. Don't be a Chicken Little, or a little chicken. Instead, pray.

Father, when I am worried, help me to trust You.

RESCUE THE FEARFUL

But when [Peter] saw the strong wind, he was afraid. He began to go down in the water. He cried out, "Lord, save me!"
MATTHEW 14:30

When we learn to swim, we all love a good floatie. They hold us up in the pool and make us feel brave while we splash in the water. We're confident when we can enjoy the water while still breathing good air.

It wasn't quite that way for Peter.

Peter watched Jesus walk on the water, and he wanted to do that too. But Peter didn't have a floatie—instead, he had Jesus, who was more than enough. When Peter trusted Jesus, he breathed good air with every miracle step he took. When Peter began to doubt, he sank. He needed help, and Jesus came to the rescue.

When you're in trouble, you know who to ask. You know that Jesus *wants* to help you out.

So walk with Him and feel brave. Trust Him and enjoy confidence. Follow Him and discover the very best adventures.

Lord Jesus, I will always need Your help. I need Your rescue. When I'm worried, You're the one I need to talk to most.

DAY 45

JOYFUL GIVING

They said to Moses, "The people are bringing much more than enough for the work the Lord told us to do."
Exodus 36:5

Moses told the people of Israel that God wanted them to build a meeting tent, also known as "the tabernacle." That was where God would meet with His people as they traveled through the desert on the way to the Promised Land. Moses asked the people to bring gold, silver, and brass, different colors of cloth, animal skins, perfume, and other things as gifts to the Lord.

Guess what? They brought so many gifts that Moses told the people to stop! What would happen in the church today if all God's people responded so generously? How many homeless people would be fed? How many needy children might get clothes? How many houses could be built?

Does this story reflect *your* attitude about giving to God? Are you willing to give so much that every need is met? Would you like to make your pastor tell the members of your church to stop giving for a while?

Lord, give me a joyful heart—one that can't wait to give You my tithes and offerings each week.

DAY 46

BRAGGING. . .ABOUT GOD

What do you have that has not been given to you?
If God has given you everything, why do you have pride?
Why do you act as if He did not give it to you?
1 Corinthians 4:7

Everything we have comes from God. If we truly believe that, then we have no right to boast about how talented we are or how much we have. Actually, we should brag about how good *God* is for giving us everything!

At times, everyone wants more—more money, more things, more friends, more popularity. But when we feel that way, we should be thankful that God has given us anything at all. The houses we live in, the people we love, the gadgets we play with, the food we eat. . .even our lives themselves are all gifts from God. Without Him, we wouldn't even exist.

Next time you feel like making yourself look good, why not make God look even better?

Dear Lord, thank You for giving me life. Thank You for taking care of my needs and even giving me extra. Help me to brag more on You than I do on myself.

DAY 47

BE CAREFUL WHAT YOU PROMISE

"When you make a promise to the Lord your God, do not be slow to pay it. It would be sin in you, for the Lord your God will be sure to ask you for it."
DEUTERONOMY 23:21

Has your dad or mom ever made a promise to you and then didn't keep it? Yes, all parents do that sometimes. Have any of your friends ever made promises to you and didn't keep them? Yes, all friends do that sometimes. When that's happened, how hard was it to forgive and forget? Yes, broken promises can hurt a lot.

That's why it's so important to be careful what *you* promise. Be careful what commitments you make to a friend. Be careful what you promise to your dad or mom. And be especially careful what you promise to the Lord your God. Breaking a promise to God is actually a sin. It's better *not* to make a promise at all than to make one and then break it.

Lord, have I made a promise to You and not kept it? I confess that breaking promises is sinful. Thank You for forgiving me.

DAY 48

BECAUSE GOD SAYS SO

"Take hope, men. I believe my God will do what He has told me."
ACTS 27:25

The apostle Paul was a man of big faith. It was the fuel that kept him going and gave him a positive attitude when times were hard.

Once, Paul was on a ship caught in a colossal storm. The waves grew larger and larger and pounded against the boat. Hoping to keep their ship from sinking, the sailors threw cargo into the sea. The storm raged on and they threw some of the sails overboard.

The sun disappeared for days. The ship's crew stopped eating. Things were really, really bad.

But Paul stood up and told everyone to hope in God. An angel had told him not to be afraid, because God would save all 276 people on the ship. And God did! When He says something, you can believe it. And always remember that God is with *you* today, just like He was with the apostle Paul.

Lord, I thank You for this story about the way You helped Paul. Help me to trust in You, even when things aren't going my way.

STAND UP FOR GOD

So stand up and do not be moved.
Wear a belt of truth around your body.
Ephesians 6:14

Do you ever feel like you're the only kid in your school or neighborhood who follows Jesus? Elijah felt the same way.

He was an Old Testament prophet of God who stood against 450 prophets of the false god Baal. Since Elijah had the truth on his side, he could challenge those false prophets to a contest. Each side would pray to their god, and the one that answered by fire would be the true god. Of course, it was Elijah's God—our God—who burned up the sacrifice and even the water that Elijah poured over the altar!

At some time or another, we'll all have to stand up for our faith. We'll need to make a decision that pleases God but almost nobody else. That will take bravery.

But the God who answered Elijah's prayer is the same God who stands by your side. In His power, you can be true and unmoved. You can stand firm!

Lord God, please give me courage to stand for Jesus in every situation. You helped Elijah, and You will help me!

GRUMPY NEIGHBORS?

Anyone who loves his neighbor will do no wrong to him. You keep the Law with love.
ROMANS 13:10

Grumpy neighbors are hard to love. They're not pleasant to talk to. They might frown if you walk too close to their yard. They could even complain to your mom or dad if they think you did something wrong.

But God says you should love people—and that includes your neighbors. And because you're supposed to love your neighbors, you shouldn't do anything to hurt them. You wouldn't intentionally annoy them. You wouldn't take anything they own. You wouldn't do anything less than treat them the way you'd like to be treated yourself. (Remember Jesus' "Golden Rule"?)

There have probably been times when *you* were hard to love too. But God's love changes people. It's possible to move from grumpy to grateful when love shows up.

Be a walking, talking example of God's love. It's how you keep His Law. It's how others come to know God's love too.

Heavenly Father, please help me to love. May I show patience, kindness, forgiveness, and care for even the grumpiest people I know.

DAY 51

INVESTING IN GOD'S KINGDOM

"He called ten of the servants he owned. He gave them ten pieces of money and said to them, 'Put this money to use until I return.'"
LUKE 19:13

When a church near Baltimore, Maryland, received an anonymous donation of ten thousand dollars, the pastor gave a hundred church members a hundred dollars each. But it wasn't for them to go shopping or out to dinner. He asked them to use the money to help others in need.

One member bought soup and socks for cancer patients. Another purchased snow pants and gloves so a child with a brain tumor could go outside and play. Some members bought Christmas presents for the homeless, and others gave money to strangers, waitresses, and bus drivers.

When Jesus gives money to His own followers, He is meeting our needs. But He also wants us to put some of that blessing to use in building His kingdom. Maybe some of those people in Baltimore now follow Jesus because a church reached out to meet their needs.

How could you use your money to invest in God's kingdom?

Lord, help me put Your money to good use until You come.

DON'T TRUST YOUR EYES

Our life is lived by faith. We do not live by what we see in front of us.
2 Corinthians 5:7

Have you ever seen a really cool magic trick? Magicians are good at making things disappear. They cut people in half and join them back together. They pull playing cards out of thin air. In reality, they are just creating illusions—that is, making it look like they can do impossible things. Magicians know that you cannot trust your eyes.

Christians aren't supposed to trust their eyes, but for a different reason. We know that this world is in God's hands. Nothing can happen that isn't part of His plan. So even when it *looks* like things are out of control, we know that that's not true. We can still trust that God knows what He's doing.

God isn't a magician who's out to trick us. He's the all-powerful God who does amazing things *because* He's God. Trust Him, even when you can't trust your eyes.

Lord, make my faith in You stronger than what I can see. Help me always trust that You have things under control.

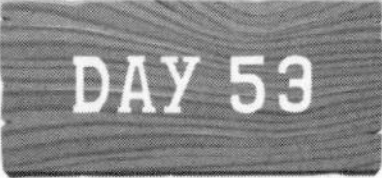

DAY 53

ANYTHING I WANT?

The Lord came to Solomon in a special dream in Gibeon during the night. God said, "Ask what you wish Me to give you."
1 Kings 3:5

Most people know Aladdin as a Disney character. But the story of a boy and his wish-granting genie in a lamp goes back hundreds of years. Everyone enjoys the idea of getting exactly what they want!

Aladdin is a fairy tale. But the Bible tells the true story of Solomon, who got to ask God for anything he wanted. What would you request? Lots of money? To be a sports star? A trip to Mars?

Here's what Solomon wanted: wisdom. As the new king of Israel, Solomon told God, "I am only a little child. . . . So give Your servant an understanding heart to judge Your people and know the difference between good and bad" (1 Kings 3:7, 9). God was so pleased with Solomon's answer that He gave the king just what he requested—*plus* money and fame.

Whatever your dreams, start by asking God for wisdom. He's happy to answer that prayer.

Father, may I boldly ask for whatever will honor You and help this world.

DAY 54

FRUSTRATING AND UNFAIR

Joseph's brothers were jealous of him.
GENESIS 37:11

Joseph had ten older brothers, and they were all jealous of him. When he told them he'd dreamed that they were bowing down to him, they were furious—and they plotted a whole bunch of trouble. You can read the whole story in Genesis 37–50. In a nutshell, the brothers sold Joseph as a slave, but years later he became the second most powerful leader in Egypt. Crazy, huh?

Well, not when you consider that "the Lord was with Joseph" (Genesis 39:2). Through every frustrating and unfair thing that Joseph went through, God was there. And God was working out every detail for His much bigger purposes.

He does that in our lives too. As the apostle Paul wrote, "We know that God makes all things work together for the good of those who love Him and are chosen to be a part of His plan" (Romans 8:28).

God knows every tough thing you face, and He's ready to make something good out of it. Your job is just to stay faithful.

Lord God, please help me to stay faithful when life seems frustrating and unfair.

FILL ME, LORD!

When they had finished praying, the place where they were gathered was shaken. They were all filled with the Holy Spirit. It was easy for them to speak the Word of God.
Acts 4:31

What would you think if the moment you finished praying your request was answered? That's what happened to some of the early Christians in the book of Acts.

They had been sharing the good news about Jesus, but the Jewish religious leaders told them to stop. The Christians were scared, but they also knew that they *had* to tell people about Jesus—no matter what anybody else said.

So they prayed, "Lord, listen to their sharp words. Make it easy for your servants to preach Your Word with power" (Acts 4:29). *Boom!* God immediately sent His Holy Spirit to fill the Christians with power. And just as they had asked, it became easy for them to speak the words of God.

When you want to tell someone about Jesus, pray for God to give you the same kind of power. He will certainly help you spread the good news!

Heavenly Father, fill me with Your Holy Spirit to speak Your words.

DAY 56

WORRY DOESN'T MAKE YOU TALLER

"Which of you can make yourself a little taller by worrying? If you cannot do that which is so little, why do you worry about other things?"
Luke 12:25–26

If worry could make us taller, some people would be bigger than mountains. If worry helped us live longer, some people might never die. If worry made us smarter, there would be really brainy people everywhere you look.

But worry doesn't do any of those good things. In fact, worry hurts us in many ways.

Worry makes it harder to remember the things God wants you to learn. Since He's taking care of you, why should you worry about things that don't make you taller, smarter, or live longer?

Nothing good ever comes from worrying. It can't change anything for the better. It can't stop any event from happening. It can't make you closer to God. So get rid of it! The way to be free from worry is to give it to God.

Lord, I don't know why it's so easy to worry but so hard to trust You. What's easy doesn't help. What's hard is the brave choice. Please help me to choose wisely.

DAY 57

THE WAY OF LIFE

You will show me the way of life. Being with You is to be full of joy. In Your right hand there is happiness forever.
Psalm 16:11

People who don't know Jesus spend their time and energy trying to discover meaning in life. Many times, they seek happiness in sinful ways and never really find lasting joy. But Jesus calls His followers to a different kind of life. He said, "My sheep hear My voice and I know them. They follow Me" (John 10:27). Jesus' sheep follow Him into eternal life.

The world says right now is all that matters. Christians live with heaven in mind. The world says you should seek joy in whatever makes you happy. Christians find joy in the Lord. The world says you have to look out for yourself. Christians know that nothing can touch them unless Jesus allows it.

Are you living with heaven in mind? Are you finding joy in the Lord? Are you trusting in the Lord for protection? If so, you have found the way of life.

Lord, I thank You for showing me the way of life! May I never stray from Your path.

IN HARD TIMES, WORSHIP GOD

We think of those who stayed true to Him as happy even though they suffered. You have heard how long Job waited. You have seen what the Lord did for him in the end. The Lord is full of loving-kindness and pity.

James 5:11

The Bible tells us that Job was a really good man. That doesn't mean he was perfect, but God was proud of him.

One terrible day, Job lost everything he owned—as well as his ten children. Can you even imagine that? Think back to a time when you lost something you really cared about: a special toy, a friend who moved to a different town, or maybe a grandparent who passed away. How did you react? Were you sad? Mad? Did you act bad?

Job reacted by worshipping God! Job 1:21 says he said, "The Lord gave and the Lord has taken away. Praise the name of the Lord." Wow!

If there's one big thing we can learn from Job, it's this: No matter how challenging life is, we should always worship God.

Lord God, please help me to worship You in every situation.

DO CHORES LIKE JESUS

"I have done this to show you what should be done. You should do as I have done to you."

JOHN 13:15

Imagine that you are a servant in Bible times. You're working in a big house in Jerusalem. To your surprise, that popular teacher Jesus comes into the house. He goes to an upper room to eat supper with His twelve apostles.

Usually a servant would wash the feet of each guest. But Jesus, smiling, takes the water bowl and towel from your hands, telling you that you're free to go do other things. You start to leave, but curiosity gets the best of you. When you turn around, you see that Jesus has knelt down and is washing an apostle's dirty feet. You can't believe it.

In today's verse, Jesus tells you to serve others. That includes doing everyday chores, even unpleasant ones. It also includes doing jobs *before* you're asked. What chore do you need to do now? Clean your room? Take out the garbage? Wash the dishes?

Father God, Jesus was more than willing to wash twenty-four stinky feet. Would You please help me to do my chores happily, like Jesus did?

"FEAR" THE LORD?

You who fear the Lord, trust in the Lord.
He is their help and safe-covering.
Psalm 115:11

Does anything make you afraid? Heights? Spiders? Speaking in front of your class? We don't like to be afraid, but some fear is actually good because it protects us. If you fall off the roof, you'll really hurt yourself. Some spiders are poisonous. You need to prepare for a speech to do it well. A certain amount of fear keeps you safe and happy.

Then there's "the fear of the Lord."

Wait—I thought God is love! Why should I be afraid of Him?

Well, there are different kinds of fear. In this verse, it's a deep respect, a kind of awe. If you feel that way about God, you can trust in Him and He will be your "help and safe-covering." This kind of fear is good—it protects you by keeping you from rebelling against God.

So don't be afraid. Just fear God!

Lord God, I want to trust You with everything in my life. Show me how to follow what You say and stay close to You every day. Be my help and safe-covering!

DAY 61

MEASURING GOD'S LOVE

Because of the blood of Christ, we are bought and made free from the punishment of sin. And because of His blood, our sins are forgiven.
EPHESIANS 1:7

How much does God love you? The Bible says that before God created the universe, He made a huge decision. He decided that Jesus Christ—God the Son—would die for your sins and for the sins of the whole world.

That incredible decision meant that Jesus, who is God in a human body, would be nailed to a rough wooden cross, experience terrible pain and suffering, and actually give up His life. He did all that to prove the full extent of God's love for you.

God loves you so much that He's forgiven your first 101 sins. Not really. The Bible says God has forgiven *all* of your sins.

Does this mean you can now sin as much as you want? No, not at all. Instead, it reminds us why we should always confess our sins to God. He'll always forgive sin because He loves you to heaven and back. You can never measure that love!

Lord, I don't understand why You love me so much, but thank You.

WALK WITH FRIENDS

All the nations may walk in the name of their god. But we will walk in the name of the Lord our God forever and ever.
Micah 4:5

Sometimes you have to stand up for what's right even when no one else makes that choice. It takes a brave boy to do that. But God doesn't want you to stand alone. Not only does He stand with you, but He might send other friends to stand with you.

Micah didn't write, "*I* will walk in the name of the Lord *my* God forever and ever." He said, "*We* will walk in the name of the Lord *our* God." That meant that Micah didn't stand alone. He didn't have to—God sent friends to stand with him.

Christian friends are a gift from God. They can help you in many ways, by encouraging good choices and reminding you that God is the one to follow.

Walk with friends who walk with God.

Lord God, You want me to walk with You, and You send me friends to encourage me on the way. I thank You for friends who also follow You.

WALKING WITH GOD

Yes, even if I walk through the valley of the shadow of death, I will not be afraid of anything, because You are with me. You have a walking stick with which to guide and one with which to help. These comfort me.
Psalm 23:4

Being brave doesn't mean you're never afraid. It just means you can move ahead with trust in God.

For most people, the scariest thing of all is death. Even Christians, who know that heaven is waiting, can find death disturbing. Everybody dies, but nobody who has died can tell you what it was like—so death is a frightening mystery.

The Bible's great psalm writer, David, described walking through "the valley of the shadow of death." Creepy, huh? But David said he wasn't afraid, because God was with Him. Like a shepherd, God carried a long stick that would keep David on the right path—and knock aside any wolves or bears that tried to attack him.

And God does the same thing for all His children. Whatever scares us is no match for Him. He's always there, always protecting.

Lord God, thanks for always being with me. I give my fears to You.

FIRE SAFETY

Have loving-kindness for those who doubt.
Save some by pulling them out of the fire.
JUDE 22–23

Have you ever toasted marshmallows over a campfire? There's an art to it: You have to rotate your stick slowly so the marshmallow toasts evenly. If it bursts into flame, just blow it out and start over.

You know, as fun as fire might seem, don't monkey around with it. Don't get too close to the flames yourself, and never mess around with other people near the fire. You have to be careful around a campfire or someone could get hurt.

Sin is a lot like fire. If you see people messing around with sin, someone will definitely get hurt. The best way to help others is to stop them from getting too close to sin in the first place. It will take bravery to stand up to people who are playing with fire, but they'll thank you for it later. No one wants to get burned.

Lord, keep me from playing with fire. And please give me the bravery I need to stop my friends from burning themselves.

DAY 65

LIGHT IN THE DARKNESS

Your Word is a lamp to my feet and a light to my path.
PSALM 119:105

Are you afraid of the dark? Lots of people are—even adults. So don't be embarrassed if dark places aren't your favorite thing.

The Bible uses the idea of darkness to describe the world we live in. Jesus said He is the "Light of the world" (John 8:12), so darkness is the opposite. Jesus is love, but the world is filled with hate. Jesus is true, but the world is full of lies. Jesus is hope and peace and joy, but the world is sad and angry and mean.

If you don't like the dark of this world, Psalm 119:105 says the Bible is a light. God's Word is like a lantern shining on a dark path. It shows us how to walk and keeps us out of troublesome places. It can even take away the fear we feel.

But the Bible won't help us unless we use it. It's like a flashlight in a drawer—we have to bring it out and let it shine!

Father in heaven, thank You for the light You shine in this dark world.

DO WHAT GOD SAYS

"Not everyone who says to me, 'Lord, Lord,' will go into the holy nation of heaven. The one who does the things My Father in heaven wants him to do will go into the holy nation of heaven."
MATTHEW 7:21

Becoming braver each day means obeying God—the first time, every time. It's easy to think we know better, but we really don't. We need to admit that only God knows everything.

Moses learned this lesson after God spoke to him through a burning bush (see Exodus 3). God said Moses would lead the Israelites out of their slavery in Egypt. But Moses couldn't believe it, and he started making excuses instead of obeying. "Who am I to lead the people?" he asked.

It took a long time—years in fact—before Moses did what God had told him to do: lead the Israelites out of their slavery. We can only imagine what would have happened had Moses obeyed God the first time.

Practice obeying God the first time, every time, even when it's hard. Then watch what great things He'll do through you!

Lord, please help me obey Your laws the first time, every time!

DAY 67

HE WILL HELP US

*"It will not be you who will speak the words.
The Spirit of your Father will speak through you."*
MATTHEW 10:20

You already know that Moses was a great leader chosen by God. And you know that he tried to get out of that job. . .crazy, huh?

One reason Moses didn't want to face the king of Egypt was because he was "slow in talking." He said, "It is difficult for me to speak" (Exodus 4:10). Sometimes we all feel that way when it comes to telling people about Jesus. But Jesus Himself made a promise, the one that we read in Matthew 10:20. When the time comes for us to speak up for Him, God the Father will give us the words.

Moses made many excuses to get out of what God asked him to do. But he forgot one of the main promises of God: If He asks us to do something, He will help us with the job!

**Father, help me to do what You want.
I know that You will help me.**

SIBLING RIVALRY

Martha was working hard getting the supper ready. She came to Jesus and said, "Do You see that my sister is not helping me? Tell her to help me."
LUKE 10:40

Sometimes the hardest people to get along with are members of our own families. We know more about them than anyone else—anyone but God. Family members know just the right words to make us mad, but they also know what we like. . .and might surprise us in ways that bring a smile.

Maybe you've heard the phrase "sibling rivalry"—that happens when two or more children in the same family just can't seem to get along. It happens, but it was never God's plan.

Jesus saw sibling rivalry up close with two sisters. When Mary didn't help out with the meal, Martha told Jesus to make her help.

Family can be a real learning experience, and brave boys make the best of it. How do you learn to get along? Speak kindly. Offer to help. Ignore careless comments. Forgive.

In time, you'll replace rivalry with respect—maybe even love.

Lord, I know that family is important to You, so please make it important to me.

BE A FRIEND

A man who has friends must be a friend,
but there is a friend who stays nearer than a brother.
Proverbs 18:24

You've probably heard the phrase "If you want to have a friend, be a friend." There's a lot of truth in that. In fact, it's just a different way of saying what today's Bible verse teaches.

Being a friend means you are willing to put the needs and feelings of others ahead of your own. It means listening to and making time for people. And it means staying by someone's side during tough times, maybe when nobody else will.

Some Bible teachers believe that the "friend who stays nearer than a brother" is actually God or Jesus—and they might be right. But that could also describe a best friend, someone who sticks with you throughout life because you care for each other so deeply.

If you're having a hard time making friends, pray about it. Ask God for help. Then take a bold chance and try to be a friend to someone.

God, help me to be the type of friend who stays nearer than a brother.

DAY 70

LOVE GOD, OTHERS. . . AND ANIMALS

Jesus said to Peter the second time, "Simon, son of John, do you love Me?" He answered Jesus, "Yes, Lord, You know that I love You." Jesus said to him, "Take care of My sheep."
John 21:16

When Dan was eleven years old, his parents let him buy two lambs. Dan and his older brother made a circular wire fence that stood up on its own. It didn't need any fence posts, so Dan could move the enclosure—and the sheep—around the lawn. Those sheep loved to eat the grass, so Dan didn't have to mow the yard anymore. He just had to take very good care of the sheep day after day.

So what does that have to do with loving God? Well, bad things happen when an animal runs out of food or water. And bad things happen when you neglect the people God has put in your life. When you care for others— whether they're animals or other people—you're showing your love for Jesus. Take care of His sheep!

Lord, I thank You that I can show my love for You by caring for others—even pets.

DAY 71

GROUP PROJECT

Since you want gifts from the Holy Spirit,
ask for those that will build up the whole church.
1 CORINTHIANS 14:12

Have you ever worked on a group project in class? If not, you will at some point, whether in middle or high school. It works like this: Each person in the group has a specific job. At the end of the project, if everyone in the group has done his or her part, the final product will be good. The teacher will be pleased.

That's kind of how things work in the church too. God has put certain people together and given them specific jobs—jobs that use the "gifts from the Holy Spirit" that 1 Corinthians 14:12 mentions. Our task is to lift other people up, to encourage them always to serve and honor Jesus. This is how we "build up the whole church." When we do that, our Teacher—Jesus Himself—will be pleased.

Sounds good, huh? Go ahead and ask God for those gifts!

Dear God, please give me gifts to build up Your church. I want to please my Teacher.

DAY 72

KEEP ON KEEPING ON

Those who keep on doing good and are looking for His greatness and honor will receive life that lasts forever.
ROMANS 2:7

Because Jesus often prayed to His Father for help, He always finished what He started. God led Him through each day of His life on earth, so Jesus never stopped in the middle of a task.

How are you doing with "keeping on"?

Each new day gives you an opportunity to do big things for God. You are special, and no one else can do the jobs He's given you. Ask Him for the strength to keep doing well with your duties at home, at school, and at church. Read your Bible to see how Jesus lived His life. As you work hard and treat people like He did, you will accomplish good things.

Be brave, and don't stop when things get hard; things will get hard sometimes. Don' trust in your own strength. Let God work through you to keep on keeping on.

Father, I want to be like Jesus. When I get tired and feel like stopping, please give me the strength to keep serving others.

DAY 73

LOVING JESUS

"But from there you will look for the Lord your God. And you will find Him if you look for Him with all your heart and soul."
DEUTERONOMY 4:29

Bruce loves the Lord with all his heart and soul. "My parents were awesome growing up," he says. "They were such good examples to me, and they always had me involved with our church. But, as you know, it doesn't matter if a kid's going to church—it's what's in your heart."

So now Bruce loves telling guys about God the Father, God the Son (Jesus Christ), and God the Holy Spirit. He loves to share about the Bible, the church, and the Christian faith. He wants other guys to love the Lord Jesus as wholeheartedly as he does.

If Bruce were sitting beside you now, here's what he would say: "Today can be that one opportunity, that one time in your life, for you to consider the Lord as your personal Savior. I pray that you do that."

Have you made that decision yet?

Lord, I thank You for what Bruce says. I want Jesus to be my Lord and Savior!

DAY 74

LIES AND EXCUSES

Then Saul said to Samuel, "I have sinned.
I have sinned against the Word of the Lord
and your words, because I was afraid of
the people and listened to them."
1 SAMUEL 15:24

Have you ever been caught doing something wrong? That's no fun, and it can make you do something else that's wrong. You might lie about the first thing you did!

That's what King Saul did. God had told Saul what he needed to do. Then Saul did something else. When the prophet Samuel asked about it, Saul lied. He made excuses. He acted like it was no big deal. But Saul finally admitted he was wrong when Samuel said God would find someone else to be king.

When you do something wrong, don't be afraid to admit that to God. He already knows what you did, and He wants to forgive you. But He's never happy with excuses and lies. One of the bravest things you can do is tell God that He was right and you were wrong.

Father, sometimes it's hard to admit I'm wrong. But I don't want to hide from You. Give me the strength to be honest with You.

GIVING ALL

[Jesus] saw a poor woman whose husband had died. She put in two very small pieces of money. He said, "I tell you the truth, this poor woman has put in more than all of them. For they have put in a little of the money they had no need for. She is very poor and has put in all she had. She has put in what she needed for her own living."

Luke 21:2–4

This poor widow dropped two "mites" into the offering. That's like you giving God your last two pennies. If you've been saving your allowance or your lawnmowing money for a while, then you have way more money than she did.

Jesus saw what this woman gave (just like He sees what everyone gives), and He praised her generosity. What does He see when you put an offering into the plate? Maybe you've been saving your money for a new video game or a skateboard. There's nothing wrong with buying new things, but are you willing to ask Jesus first if you should give some of that money to Him instead?

Lord, help me make good decisions about the money I have saved.

DAY 76

GOD'S GOT THIS!

But Moses said to the people, "Do not be afraid! Be strong, and see how the Lord will save you today. For the Egyptians you have seen today, you will never see again."
EXODUS 14:13

Do you remember the story of the Exodus—the time God's people escaped their slavery in Egypt? Moses led the Israelites out of the country, to the edge of the Red Sea. But how would they get across. . .especially with Egyptian soldiers chasing them down?

The Israelites waited by the water's edge just as God had told them to. They were afraid when they saw the soldiers coming closer. But Moses said God would fight for them. He would save the people in a way they couldn't even imagine.

That's when Moses lifted up his walking stick. The sea split in two. The people walked through on dry ground. The Egyptians rode into the sea after the Israelites, and the waters rushed back into place. Every soldier was drowned, and God's people were saved.

God can do similar things for you today. Stay positive. Don't worry. He's got this!

Lord God, may I never worry but instead trust Your goodness and power.

DAY 77

DON'T COMPLAIN

"Listen well to the voice of the Lord your God. Do what is right in His eyes. Listen to what He tells you, and obey all His Laws. If you do this, I will put none of the diseases on you which I have put on the Egyptians. For I am the Lord Who heals you."

Exodus 15:26

Moses had just led the people of Israel out of their slavery in Egypt. The Israelites had seen all the plagues God sent on Egypt. They walked across the floor of the Red Sea with the waters piled up on either side of them. They saw God do incredible things to rescue them.

Then they got thirsty and started to complain. As soon as things got a little uncomfortable, God's people got grumpy. Still, He provided water for them, reminding them that if they followed Him and did what was right, He would keep taking care of them.

When your life gets uncomfortable, do you trust God? He has promised to take care of you, just like He took care of the Israelites. Be brave, keep doing right, and don't complain.

Father God, keep me from complaining when things get tough.

DAY 78

YOUR KINGDOM COME

Jesus said to them, "When you pray, say, 'Our Father in heaven, Your name is holy. May Your holy nation come.'"
LUKE 11:2

Do you like to get your own way? Most of us sure do. But sometimes, even when we get what we want, we're still not happy. Maybe that new video game wasn't as fun as you thought it would be. Maybe you chose not to go on a family weekend trip and ended up lonely. Maybe eating a bunch of candy left you sick at your stomach. Our own way isn't always the best way.

But God's way is. That's why Jesus taught His disciples (and all of us) to pray, "Our Father in heaven. . .may Your holy nation come." Many versions of the Bible say, "May Your *kingdom* come." God is perfect, so when He is King of totally everything, everything will be totally good. And that's something we should pray for.

It takes bravery to break from the selfish ways of this world. But when we truly want what God wants, we'll find that life is better—for us and for the people around us.

Father, may Your kingdom come soon!

DAY 79

GOD DOESN'T MAKE DEALS

Give a gift of thanks on the altar to God.
And pay your promises to the Most High.
Psalm 50:14

What kinds of promises do people make to God? Soldiers on the battlefield sometimes promise to live for God if He'll keep them safe from the enemy. Those promises are often made when the bullets are actually flying. Sometimes these men keep their promises to God, but often they don't.

Does God *want* people trying to make deals with Him? No, He doesn't. Such deals won't help anyone survive, because God doesn't make deals.

Here's what God wants: action, not promises. In other words, He wants you to do what He tells you to do in the Bible. And He wants you to do the right thing *now*. Don't make promises to God to do the right thing "someday." Do what He says today and every day.

Never try to sway God into helping you just because you made some big promise. Just trust and obey Him, naturally.

Lord, I can see why soldiers try to make deals with You. Please help me to live every day for You instead.

DAY 80

HELPING GOD BY HELPING OTHERS

Religion that is pure and good before God the Father is to help children who have no parents and to care for women whose husbands have died who have troubles.
JAMES 1:27

When you know of someone in need, it's easy to think, *Someone should help them!* Maybe that "someone" is you.

It's normal to feel bad when you see a lonely kid or an older lady who lives by herself. But God doesn't just want us to feel bad—He wants us to do something. He wants us to "care for" people like that.

To do this, you'll need courage from God and maybe some help from your parents. If it's okay with them, invite a lonely kid over for dinner. Or offer to mow grass or take out the trash for a single lady down the street.

Lots of people could use a friend. Maybe God is calling you to be that friend to the needy people of your neighborhood. It's been said that Christians are Jesus' hands and feet on earth today. By helping others, you help God.

Father, please help me show Your love by encouraging sad and lonely people.

DAY 81

WAIT UNTIL THE LORD COMES

Do not be quick to say who is right or wrong. Wait until the Lord comes. He will bring into the light the things that are hidden in men's hearts. He will show why men have done these things. Every man will receive from God the thanks he should have.

1 CORINTHIANS 4:5

If your friends at school are arguing about something, don't rush to take sides. In today's verse, the apostle Paul says you should be slow to say who's right or wrong. Why? Because you can't really know what's in another person's heart, so you can't fully understand his situation. If you jump in too quickly, you might even make things worse.

But a day is coming when Jesus will make everything clear. Right now, it's not your job to decide who's right or wrong in every disagreement.

When you obey what Paul says in today's verse, you show that you trust Jesus. If you can settle a disagreement, great—do what you can to help. But if you can't, just do your best to live in peace with others.

Lord, I trust You to make everything right in the future.

DAY 82

YOU CAN EARN RESPECT

Let no one show little respect for you because you are young. Show other Christians how to live by your life. They should be able to follow you in the way you talk and in what you do. Show them how to live in faith and in love and in holy living.

1 TIMOTHY 4:12

At what age will you earn respect? When you turn sixteen and can drive a car? When you turn eighteen and are considered an adult? In today's Bible verse, the apostle Paul was talking to a good friend. We don't know how old Timothy was, but Paul called him "young." And look at what else Paul said: Timothy should not be disrespected for being young. Should he say to people, "You have to respect me"? No, Paul wanted Timothy to *earn* respect.

Like Timothy, *you* can earn respect by the way you think and talk, and by what you decide and do. Specifically, you can earn respect by trusting and obeying Jesus—and by loving other people—each and every day.

Lord, I want to earn respect day after day. To do that, I need Your help big-time!

WAITING FOR THE SON

My soul waits for the Lord more than one who watches for the morning; yes, more than one who watches for the morning.
Psalm 130:6

Thirteen-year-old Ethan stood in a field one dark fall evening. The distant city barely lit the sky, and fog was settling on the hills. Ethan couldn't wait for the sun to come up.

Suddenly, there was a horrible noise across the pasture. A wolf had come to attack Ethan's sheep! He grabbed his torch and slingshot and ran toward the sound. Soon the wolf was running away. Ethan had done what shepherds must do—protect his sheep.

Before long, the sun was rising, and Ethan's replacement arrived. Relieved, he could go home and rest.

Though Ethan was patient while he waited for the morning, he wasn't lazy. And that's exactly how God wants *us* to be: patient but also hard workers. Like a shepherd waiting for daylight to arrive, we must keep busy at our jobs while we wait.

Dear Jesus, I'm sorry for the times I've been lazy while I waited for You. Please help me to be patient but also hardworking.

DO THE RIGHT THING

He who gets things by doing wrong brings trouble to his family, but he who will not be paid in secret for wrong-doing will live.
PROVERBS 15:27

In the Bible, the Proverbs are wise sayings that can improve your life. Today's verse is a proverb that talks about doing what's right, making good choices to keep from getting into trouble.

That seems pretty basic, doesn't it? But sometimes we need reminders. Never forget that your decisions affect more than just you—if you do wrong, you'll bring trouble on your family too. But when you say no to the wrong things, you—and the people you love—do well. You won't be embarrassed by something you shouldn't have done.

Always take God seriously. He's filled His Word with both blessings and curses—good promises for the people who obey Him and bad promises for the people who do their own thing. Our lives follow the pattern of "sowing and reaping"—that means "a man will get back whatever he plants" (Galatians 6:7). Be sure you always do the right thing.

Lord God, may I always help myself and my family by obeying Your commands.

TRUTH BRINGS PEACE

*"These are the things you are to do:
Speak the truth to one another. Judge with truth
so there will be peace within your gates."*
ZECHARIAH 8:16

In Old Testament times—that is, in the centuries before Jesus was born—God's people made a lot of mistakes. A lot of big mistakes, even things like worshipping false gods. God gave them many chances to do the right thing, but they refused. Finally, God punished them by allowing invaders to wreck their country.

But God always loved His people, and through the prophet Zechariah He said that He would restore the country and its capital city, Jerusalem. God had many blessings in mind for the people, but they had to do what He wanted them to do. And what He wanted was in today's verse: They had to speak and judge truthfully. When they did that, God promised the people "peace within your gates."

In our world, some people hate the truth. It doesn't automatically bring peace. But among real Christians, truth and honesty are expected and appreciated. Speak the truth to one another!

Father, help me always to be truthful when I speak.

TICKETY-BOO

"Do not let your heart be troubled. You have put your trust in God, put your trust in Me also."
JOHN 14:1

People who live in Canada or England have a phrase they use when life is good. When they have no worries, they say "tickety-boo." Say it out loud—it's kind of fun.

God wants *you* to be tickety-boo. When troubles come your way, He doesn't want you to feel like it's the end of the world. If you can trust God, then you can trust Jesus. If you trust Jesus, then you don't have to worry about anything.

You get to decide whether or not you'll worry. But know this: If you choose to worry, it will be hard to trust God. In fact, it's *impossible* to do both at the same time. God wants you to make the choice that leaves you tickety-boo. That choice—to trust Jesus with every part of your life—will always make you closer to God and further away from worry.

Father God, help me to trust You more than I worry. I can be "tickety-boo" when I give all my concerns to You.

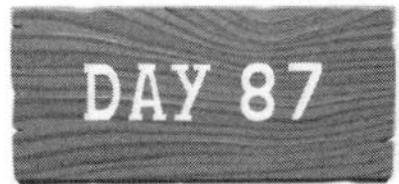

WHAT MAKES YOU HAPPY?

Be glad as you serve the Lord. Come before Him with songs of joy. Know that the Lord is God.
PSALM 100:2–3

Some people think that being a Christian takes the fun out of life. But if your faith makes you sad and boring, it's missing something.

Two hundred years ago, a Bible teacher named Adam Clarke said, "It is your privilege and duty to be happy in your religious worship. The religion of the true God is intended to remove human misery, and to make mankind happy."

We find happiness in lots of things—winning a video game, catching a big fish, scoring a basket or a touchdown. But that kind of happiness is short. True, long-term happiness comes from serving the Lord. And why not? Christians actually serve the Creator of the universe, the all-powerful, all-knowing God who spread out the stars and engineered the earth.

That kind of God doesn't *need* anything from us, but He *wants* our attention, our love, and our obedience. When we find our happiness in God, we point other people to Him too. . .and that adds to our happiness.

Lord, may I come before You with songs of joy!

DAY 88

NOT WISHFUL THINKING

Now faith is being sure we will get what we hope for. It is being sure of what we cannot see. God was pleased with the men who had faith who lived long ago.
HEBREWS 11:1–2

Imagine it's your birthday. You're about to blow out the candles when someone shouts, "Make a wish!"

Some people think faith is like believing a birthday wish will come true—but that's really called "wishful thinking." Faith is knowing *without a doubt* that the all-powerful, truthful God will do what He said He would do.

What are some of God's promises you can believe in? Well, He promises to forgive you if you confess your sins (1 John 1:9), to give wisdom when you ask for it (James 1:5), and to give you eternal life if you believe in Jesus as your Savior (John 3:16). He commands you to be strong and courageous because He will be with you wherever you go (Joshua 1:9).

When you believe God will keep His promises, He will be pleased at your faith in Him. That's a brave way to live.

Lord, You keep Your promises. Help me to claim them and live by faith in You.

BETTER TO TRUST GOD

It is better to trust in the Lord than to trust in man.
Psalm 118:8

Exactly how do we "trust in the Lord"? One way is be thankful to Him—even when things aren't working out quite the way you want them to. God is very good. When you remind yourself of that, you will build a deeper trust with Him. Remember, His love for you is forever.

Trusting God means telling Him everything that's on your heart. . .and believing that He will answer you. Don't stop trusting God when you feel worried about something, because He is your helper. Psalm 118:8 says it's better to trust God than other people. They will let you down, but God will always be there to lift you up.

As you learn to trust God, spend time telling people what He's done for you. You never know who's watching and might be encouraged by your willingness to share the truth. The more people who trust God, the better off the whole world will be. Why not start today?

Lord God, I thank You for Your goodness. Now please help me to trust You more.

MONEY!

"After a long time the owner of those servants came back. He wanted to know what had been done with his money. The one who had received the five pieces of money worth much came and handed him five pieces more. He said, 'Sir, you gave me five pieces of money. See! I used it and made five more pieces.'"

MATTHEW 25:19–20

Many guys dream of making money. They hope to play in the NBA, lead a big company, or star in blockbuster movies. . .and make millions along the way.

The Bible says, "The love of money is the beginning of all kinds of sin" (1 Timothy 6:10). But notice that it's "the *love* of money," not money itself, that causes trouble. God encourages people to work hard and earn an honest living. As you earn more and more, you'll have more and more to give to people who need help.

Whether you're mowing lawns for a few dollars a week or your rich great-grandfather left you a zillion dollars, be wise. Ask God to help you handle your money—because it really came from Him anyway.

Lord, may I stand out from this world by not loving money.

DAY 91

GOD IS READY TO FORGIVE YOU

If we tell Him our sins, He is faithful and we can depend on Him to forgive us of our sins. He will make our lives clean from all sin.
1 JOHN 1:9

Benjamin's dad had just arrived home from a business trip when he noticed a big hole in the front window. He walked up to Benjamin's room and invited him to the living room. "What can you tell me about that?"

Benjamin lowered his head and admitted that he had been fooling around, swinging a heavy toy on the end of a cord when he accidentally let go. The toy sailed right through the window and into the front yard.

He was shocked when Dad smiled and shook his hand. "Congratulations, Benjamin! You're the first kid in this family to break a window. And not just any window, but the most expensive window in the house." Then he added, "Do you think *I* ever broke any windows as a boy?"

Like Benjamin's dad, God is ready to "forgive us of our sins." Just be brave and admit them.

Lord, You already know what happened. I did it. Thank You for forgiving me.

DAY 92

YOUR GOD, MY GOD

But Ruth said, "Do not beg me to leave you or turn away from following you. I will go where you go. I will live where you live. Your people will be my people. And your God will be my God."

RUTH 1:16

You probably have someone you look up to. It could be your dad, your mom, a grandparent, or even a teacher. You pay attention to the way they do things. What they think is important to you. You want to do what they do.

In the Bible, a woman named Ruth loved her mother-in-law. Ruth wanted to follow Naomi wherever she went—and Naomi wanted to move back to the place where she was born, Bethlehem. So Ruth made the choice to follow Naomi.

You can make the choice to follow God.

Ruth made the choice to love Naomi.

You can make the choice to love God.

Ruth is remembered for her wise choices.

You can be remembered that way too. Make Naomi and Ruth's God your God.

Heavenly Father, I want to make my home with You and be part of Your family. I want You to be my God.

TRUST IN GOD, WALK IN WISDOM

He who trusts in his own heart is a fool,
but he who walks in wisdom will be kept safe.
PROVERBS 28:26

Over and over, the Bible warns against doing what seems right in our own eyes. But our sinful nature is so strong that we all need the type of warning we see above. Trusting your own heart is foolish! The world will tell you to "follow your heart," but God's Word says, "The heart is fooled more than anything else, and is very sinful" (Jeremiah 17:9).

Proverbs 28:26 says that if we "walk in wisdom," we will be "kept safe." So how do you walk in wisdom?

First, read the Bible. But don't stop there. Really study it, and meditate on it—that is, think about it whenever you can. And stay close to other Christians, especially older ones who have more experience in life, people who obey the Holy Spirit and don't trust their own desires.

Nobody does any of those things perfectly. But many people are getting better and better at them. Follow mature Christians as they trust in God and walk in wisdom.

Father, help me to walk in wisdom and be safe.

DAY 94

ASKING FOR GIFTS

"You are bad and you know how to give good things to your children. How much more will your Father in heaven give good things to those who ask Him?"
MATTHEW 7:11

Kids always ask a parent or guardian or favorite aunt for special things. We want an ice cream cone or a new shirt or a cool book we saw at the store. Adults don't always give us what we want, but many times they do. They like to be generous and make us happy.

Jesus said God the Father is the same way—if we ask for "good things." Of course, it's possible to ask for bad things, things that might hurt us or interfere with other people's well-being. But if we ask God for wisdom, strength, and maybe even money for helping others, He's going to be like the adults in our lives. . .happy to give.

Sometimes God will say no to our requests. He knows there are times we might misuse what we ask for. But if you see needs you'd like to help with, ask God to provide. He gives good things!

Lord, please give me what I need for helping others.

LEARNING THE HARD WAY

Someone said to Jesus, "Your mother and brothers are standing outside. They want to see You." Jesus said to them, "My mother and brothers are these who hear the Word of God and do it."

Luke 8:20–21

Jesus said you're an important part of His family when you hear *and obey* God's Word. Jonah learned that lesson the hard way.

God had called Jonah to preach in the big, scary city of Nineveh. Jonah thought, *No way!* But God loved those wicked, violent people and wanted them to be saved.

Jonah not only disobeyed God, he ran in the opposite direction. But while he was on his getaway ship, a huge storm blew up. Jonah realized God was getting his attention.

You probably know the story: Jonah jumped overboard and was swallowed by a giant fish. He spent three days in the fish's stomach before being spit out on shore—and then he finally obeyed God by preaching in Nineveh.

It was a tough lesson, but there was a happy ending: Many people were saved when Jonah did what God said.

Lord, please help me to study Your Word and do what it says!

LET PEOPLE KNOW

"O give thanks to the Lord. Call upon His name. Let the people know what He has done."
1 Chronicles 16:8

The apostle Paul traveled all over the Roman Empire, telling others about Jesus. On his first trip, Paul knew no one. But through the power of the Holy Spirit, he started churches.

Paul made three of these "missionary journeys," some that lasted for years. He walked and sailed thousands of miles to share the gospel in places like Corinth, Thessalonica, Philippi, and Galatia. And he wrote some very important letters to encourage their churches. (Those letters are now "books" in the New Testament.)

Can you imagine walking thousands of miles, over several years, for *anything*? Or being shipwrecked, thrown in prison, and pelted with stones? Through it all, Paul kept going, driven to share the connection to God that anyone can have through Jesus.

Is God calling you anywhere to tell people about Jesus? Do you have fellow students or neighbors who need to know Him? Be like Paul—let people know what God has done for you.

Father, show me where I should go to tell what Jesus has done for me.

DAY 97

GOD SMILES WHEN YOU SERVE

"For sure, I tell you, anyone who gives a cup of cold water to one of these little ones because he follows Me, will not lose his reward."
MATTHEW 10:42

On a hot day, have you ever seen someone playing or working or standing around who looked thirsty? Have *you* ever been that super thirsty guy? If someone gave you a nice cold glass of water or juice to drink, you'd probably be pretty happy. You'd probably smile.

In today's Bible verse, Jesus says that when you serve anyone—even a little kid—you'll get a reward. That's probably something special in heaven, beyond just the enjoyment you get from helping out here. And the serving can be as simple as giving someone a juice box or a cold can of pop. Who knew?

Next time you're going out, why not prepare for a little serving? Take along a cold drink for yourself. . .and for someone else. You'll make *God* smile.

Lord Jesus, when You were a boy, did anyone give You a cup of cold water? I'd like to serve You in that way by serving the people around me.

DAY 98

THE WAY GOD SAYS

Then Abraham said to God,
"If only Ishmael might live before You!"
GENESIS 17:18

It's easy to *say* that God always keeps His promises. But sometimes it's hard to *believe* that.

God made Abraham a promise, and it was a big one: Abraham would have a son, and this son would be the beginning of a whole nation of people!

But Abraham was in his eighties, and more than ten years had passed since God made His promise. Abraham got tired of waiting, so he made a plan of his own. He had a son named Ishmael.

As Ishmael grew, Abraham asked if God would bless the boy. God did bless Ishmael but told Abraham to be patient—He had a different, better plan. The son God had promised would be called Isaac, and Abraham only had to wait another year to have him.

Dads want the best for their children. Abraham did. God does. And someday, if you become a dad, you'll want the best for your kids too. Whatever the case, it's important to do what God says, *the way He says.*

God, help me to obey Your commands, knowing that Your promises always come true.

KEEP YOUR FAMILY FRIENDS

Do not leave your own friend or your father's friend alone.
Proverbs 27:10

King Solomon had a friend named Hiram, the king of Tyre. Hiram had also been friends with Solomon's dad, King David. When Solomon began to build God's temple in Jerusalem, he asked Hiram to supply the lumber and some of his workers. Hiram was happy to help. You can read about this in 1 Kings 5.

Sadly, when Solomon's son Rehoboam became king, he didn't value this family friendship. Instead, 1 Kings 12:8 says, "Rehoboam turned away from the wise words the leaders [who worked with his father] gave him. Instead he spoke with the young men who grew up with him and stood by him." He ended up losing his kingdom.

Do your parents have longtime friends who've always seemed to be there for your family? As you grow up, don't leave those friends behind. They will always be happy to help you and give you advice. You can certainly make your own friends, but your parents' friends are important too. Honor them and see how God can use them in your life.

God, I thank You for giving my family good friends.

IMPOSSIBLE PROBLEMS

One of His followers was Andrew, Simon Peter's brother. He said to Jesus, "There is a boy here who has five loaves of barley bread and two small fish. What is that for so many people?"

John 6:8–9

When you're faced with a big problem, you may be tempted to give up before you begin. Jesus' disciples did that when He asked them to get food for thousands of hungry people.

One disciple spoke up to say they didn't have enough money to feed a crowd that large. Andrew, another disciple, found a boy with five loaves of bread and two small fish—but he knew it wasn't possible to feed everyone with that.

Jesus *loves* impossible situations, though—because they allow Him to show His power. When the boy offered up his lunch, Jesus gave thanks to God the Father and started handing out bread and fish, bread and fish, and *more* bread and fish to the crowd. In the end, everyone ate as much as they wanted. . .and there were twelve baskets left over!

When a problem feels impossible, give it to Jesus and watch Him work.

Lord, show me that all things are possible with You.

DON'T GIVE UP

Do not let yourselves get tired of doing good. If we do not give up, we will get what is coming to us at the right time.
GALATIANS 6:9

Can you imagine getting tired of doing the right thing? It's possible. Even the Bible talks about that.

When the apostle Paul wrote a letter to Christians in a place called Galatia, he urged them to keep doing good no matter how hard it was. He wanted them to help each other through their problems. He told them to stay humble, and never to think of themselves as more important than anyone else. And he warned them against comparing themselves with each other. When we worry about who's smarter or richer or better looking, we won't be helping people the way God wants us to.

If everyone does right, life is smoother and happier. But many people do the wrong things—and that can make life tough. But keep doing good. Don't give up. Someday, God will reward you big-time.

God, sometimes I get tired of helping others. Please give me strength to do what You want me to do—and remind me of Your coming reward!

HOW TO LOOK FOR GOD

Look for the Lord and His strength.
Look for His face all the time.
Psalm 105:4

If you wanted to see the Lord's face today, where would you look? Well, you could open your Bible to Psalm 105 and find that the verse after today's scripture says, "Remember the great and powerful works that He has done. Keep in mind what He has decided and told us" (Psalm 105:5).

In other words, if you want to see the Lord's face today, you can look at nature. No, nature isn't God! But the Lord God made heaven and earth. (You can read that in the very first verse of the Bible.) When you look at nature, then, you can see what God is like.

First, nature tells us that the Lord God is amazingly powerful. Second, He has created untold billions of interesting things for us to see—on land, in the ocean, and overhead in the sky. Best of all? He gives us those things to enjoy!

Lord, when I see the amazing things
You have made, I feel like saying, "Wow!"
Thank You for giving us such an incredible world.

BRIGHT EYES, BRAVE HEART

The Laws of the Lord are right, giving joy to the heart.
The Word of the Lord is pure, giving light to the eyes.
Psalm 19:8

You don't have to live very long to realize that this world is a hard place. Teachers can be unfair. Friends don't always treat you right. People you love get sick and die. And many terrible things happen to other people—earthquakes, terrorism, plane crashes. How can you stay positive in a world like that?

Open your Bible. Read it. Think it over. Do that again and again.

The Bible helps us make sense of this crazy world. And it shows us that God has a plan to fix things. First, He'll save people's souls when they believe in Jesus. Then someday, He'll remake the whole world and Jesus will be King forever.

The better we know God's Word, the better we know God and His plans. And that will give us bright eyes and brave hearts in a world that really needs them.

Heavenly Father, please speak to me through Your Word. I want to have joy. And I want others to see that joy in my face.

A BETTER PLAN

The fear of man brings a trap, but he who trusts in the Lord will be honored.
PROVERBS 29:25

A popular boy in school gets a new video game. It cost his parents a lot of money. He makes sure everybody knows that he thinks only the most important kids in school own that game. How does that make you feel?

Would you be afraid if he asked you if *you* own the game? Would it seem unfair because all the boys who have the same game agree with Mr. Popular? What if they all made fun of you because you couldn't afford the game?

God says that that kind of fear is a trap. And He says that trusting Him brings more honor than following some person who makes temporary rules about unimportant things.

Sometimes, being brave means not paying attention to what's popular so you can follow God instead. He always has better plans for your life anyway.

God, sometimes I really want what other boys have. I want to be like them and accepted. But You've given everything to accept me. It's always more important to be like You.

DAY 105

THE RIGHT RESPONSE TO SALVATION

Zaccheus stood up and said to the Lord,
"Lord, see! Half of what I own I will give to poor people.
And if I have taken money from anyone in a wrong
way, I will pay him back four times as much."
LUKE 19:8

Zaccheus was a high-level tax collector—and he was rich. We don't know for sure how he got all his money, but many tax collectors were known for cheating people. Luke 19:7 says other people called Zaccheus a "sinner." But when he heard that Jesus was headed his way, Zaccheus felt like he had to see Him.

After he met Jesus, Zaccheus offered to give half of all he owned to the poor—as well as paying back four times the amount to anybody he had cheated. Now, don't think Zaccheus was trying to earn forgiveness from Jesus—nobody can do that. But when Jesus forgives us freely, we should respond with all we have. Forgiven people are generous with their time and money.

How generous have you been since you've become a Christian?

Lord, now that You've saved my soul, please make me as generous as Zaccheus.

THE BEST TRANSLATOR

In the same way, the Holy Spirit helps us where we are weak. We do not know how to pray or what we should pray for, but the Holy Spirit prays to God for us with sounds that cannot be put into words.
Romans 8:26

Have you heard of Dr. Dolittle? He's a character in a series of children's books, a veterinarian who can understand and speak the language of any animal he meets. Wouldn't that be an amazing skill to have?

Animals in the Dr. Dolittle stories need a translator because they can't tell human beings what they're feeling. In some ways, the Holy Spirit does the same work between us and God. When you struggle to pray—when nothing comes to mind or it's hard to concentrate—the Holy Spirit helps out. He "translates" our prayers to God in the exact way we meant to say them.

If you don't know what to pray for or feel like you might have said the wrong thing in a prayer, don't be discouraged. Thanks to the Holy Spirit, God hears your prayers perfectly. Just keep praying!

God, I thank You for Your Holy Spirit's help in prayer.

HOLDING HANDS

"For I am the Lord your God Who holds your right hand, and Who says to you, 'Do not be afraid. I will help you.'"
Isaiah 41:13

Can you imagine God holding your hand? That's exactly what He told the prophet Isaiah that He does.

God wants you to understand that you mean the world to Him. He made you, and He has plans for your life. That's pretty cool when you stop and think about it.

God has promised that He will never turn away from you. He will protect you. He will give you strength and help you. All of those promises are for *you*. Plant them in your heart, and you'll grow a good, positive attitude as you live life each day.

Whether you're at home or school or anywhere else, God is watching over you. He cares about all the things you care about. He has the wisdom and the power and the desire to see you through all your challenges.

So let Him hold your hand. And don't forget to say, "Thanks!"

Lord, show me how to keep a positive attitude. Fill me with Your peace every day.

TOO MUCH TALK

It is better not to make a promise,
than to make a promise and not pay it.
ECCLESIASTES 5:5

Have you ever heard someone who talked too much? Was that someone ever *you*? The Bible often warns against careless speaking, about saying things that shouldn't be said.

Ecclesiastes 5:5 is part of a group of verses (called a "passage") that warn against "empty words"—you might say, *blabbing*. According to this passage, fools come "with many words" (verse 3). Your mouth can "cause you to sin" (verse 6). It's better to listen than to talk (verse 1).

Those things are certainly true if you're making careless promises. Today's verse says it's better never to make a promise than not to live up to a promise you do make. Why is that such a big deal to God? Because He always fulfills His promises—and He wants us to be like Him.

The people of this world like to talk, talk, talk. They boast about themselves, they criticize others, they make promises they'll never keep. Being different takes bravery—but that's how you please God. Avoid too much talk.

Father, help me to speak less and listen more.

DO WHAT YOU CAN

If a man is ready and willing to give, he should give of what he has, not of what he does not have.
2 CORINTHIANS 8:12

Brave boys want to help others. But sometimes the needs are so big, you think, *What can I possibly do?*

Maybe a missionary tells your church that Africa or India or South America needs a new hospital. It will cost a million dollars. Yikes! What can *you* do?

The apostle Paul says you should just do what you can. You don't need to give a million bucks that you don't have. But you could give a single dollar that you do have. If there are 999,999 other brave boys willing to give a dollar, that hospital will get built!

Everything you have comes from God. He allows you to use most of it, just asking you to share the rest with people in need. The great thing is that He doesn't expect you to meet *every* need in the world. Do what *you* can, then see how *He* makes things happen!

Lord, may I be generous with the money You've given me. Please make it do great things.

DAY 110

THE LOVE RESPONSE

"I say to you who hear Me, love those who work against you. Do good to those who hate you. Respect and give thanks for those who try to bring bad to you. Pray for those who make it very hard for you."

LUKE 6:27–28

Jesus spoke about the worst things people do, then told you how to respond. When other people work hard to keep you from achieving your goals, love them. When people hate you, do good in return. When they try to get you in trouble, give thanks. When they make life difficult, pray for them.

Who could do that? It sounds impossible.

Well, Jesus didn't ask you to do something that had never been done before. *He* loved, *He* did good, *He* gave thanks, and *He* prayed when He was betrayed, hurt, and killed. Now He wants you to do what He did when people were against Him.

Ask Jesus for help and follow His example. Show His "love response" to everyone.

Lord, this seems so hard—but You loved those who hated You. Help me, and I will do my best to show Your love.

THE GREAT HOPE

We are to be looking for the great hope and the coming of our great God and the One Who saves, Christ Jesus.
Titus 2:13

Have you ever looked forward to a special event? Maybe you couldn't wait to ride the roller coasters at your favorite amusement park. Or maybe you were eager to see your school friends at a classmate's birthday party. Maybe you were itching to play in your team's big game. Anticipating something makes it even more enjoyable when the event actually happens.

The same is true in our Christian lives. In today's verse, the apostle Paul says we should be looking for the "great hope"—Jesus' second coming to earth. Galatians 5:5 mentions this great hope as well and gives us a clearer understanding of what it means: "We are waiting for the hope of being made right with God. This will come through the Holy Spirit and by faith."

When Jesus returns to earth, He's going to make everything right. Sadness, sickness, death—all of those things will be finished! So go ahead and think about your own special events. But spend even more time thinking about Jesus' return.

Come, Lord Jesus.

DAY 112

LOVING-PITY?

God has chosen you. You are holy and loved by Him. Because of this, your new life should be full of loving-pity. You should be kind to others and have no pride. Be gentle and be willing to wait for others.

Colossians 3:12

What does it mean to be "full of loving-pity" for others? Normal pity looks at another person and feels sorry for him—sorry that he isn't as good as you are. Loving-pity looks at another person and loves him, regardless of how bad he might be. When you have loving-pity, you don't compare another person to yourself, because love doesn't allow you to think about yourself.

Remember, our perfect God saw you with all your problems and still rescued you from sin—not because He felt sorry for you, but because He loves you.

So when you see someone with problems, don't look down on him. Lift him up. He doesn't need someone to feel sorry for him. He needs someone to love him as a friend, to be gentle and patient with him. If God could do that for you, you can do it for others.

Lord, help me love others as You have loved me.

GOODBYE, LAZINESS

When men are lazy, the roof begins to fall in.
When they will do no work, the rain comes into the house.
ECCLESIASTES 10:18

When people work out at the gym, they get stronger and healthier. It's the same with your spiritual life. If you read your Bible and talk to God every day, you build stronger spiritual muscles. Those "exercises" help keep your thoughts focused on truth. When we're lazy spiritually, we run the risk of wandering away from God. And where we end up, nothing good happens.

The Bible often warns against laziness. We're told that we should imitate the hardworking ants (Proverbs 6:6–8), that laziness leads to being poor (Proverbs 6:1–11), and that people who won't work shouldn't be given food (2 Thessalonians 3:10). And today's verse shows that laziness leads to bigger problems—like the roof of your house collapsing!

Decide today to say goodbye to laziness. With God's strength, you can work hard and bring Him glory.

Lord Jesus, it's easy for me to get lazy and not give my best effort. Help me to work hard at everything I do, whether that's mowing the grass or studying Your Word.

YOUR FAITH MATTERS!

Because Abel had faith, he gave a better gift in worship to God than Cain. His gift pleased God. Abel was right with God. Abel died, but by faith he is still speaking to us.

HEBREWS 11:4

Do you know the story of Cain and Abel? Ugh, Cain *murdered* his brother Abel. That was terrible, of course, but not the end of the story.

According to today's verse, Abel put his faith in God. He worshipped God. He gave gifts and offerings to God. Abel wasn't perfect, but God forgave Abel's sins. He was "right with God," and after he died, he went to paradise. Someday, you're going to meet Abel in heaven.

If Abel were here right now, he might say, "Don't worry about me. I'm fine! Heaven is incredible. Never stop believing in God. Never stop obeying Him. Always remember that your faith matters."

Faith—belief and trust in God—is what pleases Him (Hebrews 11:6). You bet your faith matters!

Lord, I have put my faith and trust in You. I want to live for You, worship You, and please You. Help me to stay strong in my faith. . .I know it matters.

KING OF THE JUNGLE?

There is hope for the one who is among the living. For sure a live dog is better off than a dead lion.
Ecclesiastes 9:4

Whether or not you've taken a safari to Africa, you've seen lions—maybe in a zoo, or on TV, or pictured in a book. Lions are impressive, and we'd all like to be as strong and confident as they are.

But even "the king of the jungle" has his limits. The Bible says that a dead lion is no better than any live dog. (Imagine a shivering poodle!) That's because with life, there's hope. No matter how weak we might feel, God can make us strong. No matter how confused we are, God can give us wisdom. No matter how tough things seem, God will always be with us.

You don't have to be the strongest, most confident guy in your school, or neighborhood, or world. Just know that God's strength and confidence are yours whenever you need them. All you have to do is ask.

Father, I'm thankful that I don't have to be "king of the jungle." May I always remember that You are the King of the universe.

TAKEN CARE OF

"Think how the flowers grow. They do not work or make cloth. Yet, I tell you, that King Solomon in all his greatness was not dressed as well as one of these flowers. God puts these clothes on the grass of the field. The grass is in the field today and put into the fire tomorrow. How much more would He want to give you clothing?"
LUKE 12:27–28

King Solomon was a very wise king. He was also rich and famous. He could have the best clothes made at any time. But Jesus said that the wildflowers were dressed better than King Solomon. The fields looked better in a blanket of grass than this famous human king in all his fancy clothes. And even though these plants are eventually gathered and burned, God still makes sure they're beautiful.

You may not think much about grass and flowers, but God does. And He wants you to understand that He takes care of every living thing. He takes care of the flowers and grass—and *He takes care of you.*

Lord God, You made me and take care of me. You must really love me!

SUFFERING. . .HAPPILY?

So the missionaries went away from the court happy that they could suffer shame because of [Jesus'] Name.
Acts 5:41

It may sound strange, but the Bible says suffering can actually make us happy. Nobody wants to be made fun of, left out, or beaten up. But many people have faced that kind of treatment for following Jesus. And—amazingly—they came out of it happy!

In today's verse, Peter and "the missionaries" (the other apostles) were beaten for teaching about Jesus. Another time, Paul and Silas were thrown in jail for preaching the gospel (Acts 16). Other early Christians had their things taken from them for following Jesus (Hebrews 10:34). And all of them were happy that they could suffer for Jesus' name.

The United States has usually been a safe place for Christians, but today there's more harassment and mockery than ever. Are you ready to be teased (or worse) for following Jesus? Remember: If you're faithful to Him, He'll be faithful to you—you really can't lose. In fact, you can even face suffering for Him happily.

Lord Jesus, give me strength to stand for You, no matter what.

DAY 118

TELL THE TRUTH, EVEN UNDER PRESSURE

So stop lying to each other. Tell the truth to your neighbor. We all belong to the same body.
EPHESIANS 4:25

In the book *The Lion, the Witch, and the Wardrobe*, a little girl hiding in a clothes cabinet discovers the entrance to a magical world called Narnia.

When Lucy, the youngest of four children, tells her older siblings, they think she's only playing a game. Later, her brother Edmund discovers Narnia too, even meeting Lucy in the place of wonder. But when Lucy tells the older children about her adventure with Edmund, he lies, saying he had never been there. Edmund does not want to be considered a little kid like Lucy. Not surprisingly, the lie damages Edmund's relationship with Lucy.

Sometimes we're all tempted to say something untrue, thinking that will protect us from trouble or embarrassment. But the truth is that lying always causes more harm than good. Since Jesus is "the Truth" (John 14:6), honor Him by telling the truth—even under pressure.

Lord Jesus, in those moments when I am afraid and want to lie, help me to stand firm and tell the truth.

SOLID FOUNDATION

"Trust in the Lord forever. For the Lord God is a Rock that lasts forever."
ISAIAH 26:4

Have you ever seen a new building under construction? The first thing to "go up" is actually "way down"—the foundation. Machines dig out a trench that's filled with heavy-duty concrete. When that's rock hard, the rest of the house can be built on top of it. Without a solid foundation, the building would eventually wobble and fall down.

The Bible says God is a rock. He's like a strong, unmoving foundation that you can build your life on. Other people chase money and fame and fun—things that don't last forever and can't save your soul. But brave boys know that life is all about God. When you read His Word, learn His ways, and choose to follow His plan, you are building a solid life that will stand forever. You won't wobble and fall down when hard times come.

The world will tell you to build on other foundations, but they're all like sand on a seashore. Settle yourself on the Rock—God—and you'll never be sorry.

Lord, may I put into practice everything I learn in Your Word.

WAITING ON THE PROMISE

Abraham was willing to wait and God gave to him what He had promised.
HEBREWS 6:15

Did you ever have to wait a long time for something you really wanted? Well, Abraham had to wait *a hundred years* to have his son Isaac. Can you imagine? God promised to give Abraham a child—and because God promised, Abraham waited. Patiently.

The truth is, waiting for things that seem really far away is tough. It's safe to assume that Abraham sometimes struggled with waiting, because he really wanted to be a dad! But when God says He'll do something, He does it—and it's awesome.

Just as God promised Abraham a son, He promised everyone that He would send His own Son to save us—and He did. Then He promised that His Son would come again to take His followers home to heaven—and you can be sure He will.

God didn't say exactly *when* Jesus will come to get us, but He does tell us to wait patiently. That day is going to be incredible!

Dear Lord, help me to remember that Your promises are worth waiting for. Amen.

FORGIVING OTHERS WHEN THEY DON'T ASK

"When you stand to pray, if you have anything against anyone, forgive him. Then your Father in heaven will forgive your sins also."
MARK 11:25

Saturday morning was sunny. Steve couldn't wait to head over to his best friend's house. Except when he went out the back door, his expensive twelve-speed bicycle was gone. Someone had used heavy-duty wire cutters, since all that was left was the broken chain and lock.

Steve couldn't believe it. Why would anyone steal *his* bike? Well, because it was worth a lot, he realized. Worst of all? Steve hadn't written down the serial number. As a result, it would be much harder to get his bike back. It was long gone.

Steve was angry and yelled at the dog, who whimpered and ran. Then he felt even worse. "Lord," he prayed, "I'm sorry for yelling at my dog. And I forgive whoever it was that stole my bike."

Sometimes we just have to give our anger and sadness to God. Forgive others—and trust Him to deal with them.

Lord, it's hard to forgive people who do us wrong. But help me to do what Jesus commands.

A VERSE ABOUT BULLIES

Do not be jealous of a man who hurts others,
and do not choose any of his ways.
PROVERBS 3:31

Would you need someone to tell you what to look for in a bully? Probably not. You've seen them, and they aren't very much fun to be around. You've heard them, and their words aren't kind.

God made sure that the Bible contains verses about bullies, and it's clear what He thinks. He doesn't want *you* to be like a bully. If they are rude, choose kindness instead. If they pick on others, choose to encourage. If they are harsh, choose gentleness.

Being a bully is never a good idea. They can't obey God because they don't make a choice to love others. And love is God's greatest command.

God actually loves bullies. But He wants them to accept His love and then share it with others. He wants bullies to see that the way they act isn't the way He acts. It should never be the way you act.

Lord, help me to remember that anyone who has made bad choices can change their ways—with Your help.

TRUST IN THE NAME OF THE LORD

Some trust in wagons and some in horses.
But we will trust in the name of the Lord, our God.
Psalm 20:7

David might have written Psalm 20 as a prayer set to music, something that he and his soldiers sang before they went to war. They might have looked across the battlefield to see an enemy with many wagons and horses. But they could proclaim that they trusted the Lord more than any other thing.

If anyone had reason to be confident going into a fight, it would've been David. He was known for having killed tens of thousands of men on the battlefield (1 Samuel 18:7). But David's confidence wasn't in himself. It was in the name of the Lord, His God.

You have spiritual battles going on all around you. Some of your family and friends are unbelievers. The whole world is an angry, unhappy, godless place. There's no way you can change things yourself—but you don't have to! Trust in the name of the Lord your God, knowing that He can win any battle.

Lord, please break through the spiritual barriers in the lives of my friends and relatives.

YOUR SUPERPOWER

Every child of God has power over the sins of the world. The way we have power over the sins of the world is by our faith.
1 John 5:4

Wouldn't it be cool to have a superpower? It's fun to imagine what life would be like if you could fly or had super strength. But every child of God has a superpower already. Really! By faith, you have power over the sins of the world.

Maybe that doesn't sound like a superpower to you. But just imagine a world free from sin. No one would have to worry about criminals stealing things. There would be no more murder or violence. People would keep their promises and treat everyone else with respect. If that doesn't sound like something a superhero fights for, what does?

God conquered sin when Jesus died on the cross. If you are tempted to do something you shouldn't, ask God for help and He will give you the strength to fight the temptation. You can make this world a better place by using the power God gives you over the sins of the world.

Lord, help me fight off temptation with Your super strength.

PETER'S BRAVE TURNAROUND

Then Peter and the missionaries said,
"We must obey God instead of men!"
Acts 5:29

Peter was one of Jesus' closest friends. But after Jesus had been arrested and put on trial, Peter lost his courage and pretended to not even *know* Him.

He was ashamed of himself, but Jesus forgave Peter and told him to keep telling others how to be saved. Peter obeyed and kept preaching the gospel. In fact, one time when he spoke in Jerusalem, three thousand people believed!

And Peter kept standing up for Jesus. The Jewish religious leaders were jealous and didn't want people following Jesus, so they arrested Peter (and some of Jesus' other disciples) and threw them into prison. The religious leaders told Jesus' followers to stop sharing the gospel, but Peter and his friends answered with the words of today's verse: "We must obey God instead of men!"

Peter had made some big mistakes in his life, but he served a forgiving God. So do you. Don't let your mistakes keep you down. God still wants to do good things through you!

Lord, please help me to be brave and tell people about Jesus, just like Peter did.

PRAISE WHEN SAVED

Let the people who have been saved say so.
He has bought them and set them free from
the hand of those who hated them.
PSALM 107:2

Most everyone knows the story of David and Goliath. A young Israelite—just a shepherd boy—defeats an enormous, experienced Philistine soldier in battle.

But that was only one of the many victories God gave David. As a boy he had defended his flocks of sheep against bears and lions. As a king, he led many successful military efforts. Somehow, in the midst of all his other duties, the poetic and musical David wrote many of the psalms in our Bibles today.

"I call to the Lord," he once sang, "Who has the right to be praised. And I am saved from those who hate me" (Psalm 18:3).

Hopefully, we don't have the kind of enemies David did. But when we need help, we should follow his example in calling out to God. Then, after He's helped us, we should tell others what God has done so they can share in our joy.

Father, I thank You for helping me, no matter what situation I find myself in.

WHEN YOU'RE STUCK

We wanted to come to you. I, Paul, have tried to come to you more than once but Satan kept us from coming.
1 Thessalonians 2:18

Sometimes you have good plans, but they just don't work out. Maybe your dream is to do great things, but it just falls flat. Why does that happen?

The apostle Paul has an answer: Our enemy, Satan, works hard to stop us from doing good. Paul was one of the greatest Christians of all time, and not even his plans were guaranteed. We shouldn't expect that our own dreams will happen easily—if they happen at all.

If that sounds like a bummer, consider this: The devil can only do what God allows him to do. So if Satan is keeping you from some good work, it's really because God has other plans for you. And God's plans are always the best plans.

Keep that in mind whenever you feel stuck.

Heavenly Father, I thank You for directing my dreams. I'll praise You for giving me success in them, and I'll praise You for the times when You steer me to other things. May I accept whatever plan You have for me.

DAY 128

ON TARGET

The children of a young man are like arrows in the hand of a soldier.
PSALM 127:4

Have you ever used a bow and arrow? The Bible says *you* are an arrow. King Solomon, who wrote Psalm 127, might have remembered shooting arrows with his dad, David. He was inspired to use a bow and arrow to talk about brave parents and their boys, and a good future.

Just like soldiers shoot their arrows carefully, parents wisely aim their children. You wouldn't expect a soldier to just pull back the bowstring and zing an arrow into the sky. He carefully aims the arrow, letting it fly only when he has the target in sight.

There should always be a reason for a warrior to shoot an arrow. That's the responsibility God gives moms and dads with their own boys. Parents train their children, aiming them at the target God has set. . .and, at just the right time, send them out on the adventure of life.

God, it's good to know You have a future for me. Guide me. Guide my family. Help me make the right choice to go where You send me.

IRON SHARPENS IRON

Iron is made sharp with iron, and one man is made sharp by a friend.
PROVERBS 27:17

If you've ever seen someone sharpen a knife, you might remember what is called a "honing steel." It looks like a mini-sword, only the blade is round and feels like a file. As you rub a knife blade back and forth against the honing steel, it becomes sharp again.

This is what the Christian life is supposed to look like: One Christian guy is open and honest with another Christian friend about what is going on in his life. Then he listens carefully to his friend, who might offer advice or suggest a Bible passage to read. Or the second guy might pray with his friend. Friends help each other to figure out the best way to obey Jesus. The Bible calls this being sharpened.

If you don't already have a close Christian friend, start looking! Ask God for someone you can count on to sharpen you spiritually. The Christian life was not meant to be lived alone.

Lord, send me a Christian friend so we can sharpen each other.

DAY 130

JESUS STILL HEALS TODAY

Jesus went away from the Jewish place of worship and went into Simon's house. Simon's mother-in-law was in bed, very sick. They asked Jesus to help her. He stood by her and told the disease to leave. It went from her. At once she got up and cared for them.

LUKE 4:38–39

A lot of us hate being around someone who's sneezing and blowing his nose every two minutes. But Jesus was different. That's right—as God's Son, He could (and still can) heal anyone. And when He was here on earth, He did just that.

Jesus didn't just heal grown-ups like Simon Peter's mother-in-law. He also healed boys and girls who were sick and dying. He even brought a twelve-year-old girl and an older boy back from the dead.

Do you know anyone who is sick? If so, Jesus can use *you*. How? Well, you can pray for that person's healing. The Lord can't wait to hear and answer that kind of prayer—a prayer of strong faith. Go for it!

Lord, I believe You can heal anyone of anything. Help me to pray in faith for the healing of sick people I know.

HOLD ON TO TRUTH

But as for you, hold on to what you have learned and know to be true.
2 Timothy 3:14

Once you've learned the truth of God's Word, it will take bravery to hold on to it. Why? Because many, many people will fight God's truth.

But that's nothing new. Almost two thousand years ago, the apostle Paul urged his young friend Timothy to stand for the truth. Paul warned Timothy that some people would love themselves and money much more than they loved God. Some people would boast about themselves, mistreat their parents, chase after pleasure, and insult God. If you've noticed, we live in a world like that too.

But God has something much better for His children. He offers love, joy, peace, and all kinds of good things to those who will "hold on to what you have learned and know to be true." No, it's not easy to stand against the whole world, but don't forget that you have God on your side. And nothing can stand against Him!

Father God, please help me to read my Bible, hold on to what I learn, and be true to You.

HOW LONG?

Lips that tell the truth will last forever,
but a lying tongue lasts only for a little while.
PROVERBS 12:19

Can you think of a time that you lied? How did that work out? Did it seem to help you for a while? Did the lie cause trouble in the long run?

God's Word often tells us to speak the truth. That's probably because Jesus is called "the Truth" (John 14:6), and the apostle Paul tells us that God "cannot lie" (Titus 1:2). Ever since Satan ruined the world with his lie to Eve (see Genesis 2), human beings have had problems with the truth. But no matter how tough it may be to speak honestly, that's what God wants us to do.

Today's verse offers both a promise and a warning. Truthfulness is part of the Christian life, which lasts forever. Lies die with us, in our short life on earth.

Which sounds better to you? Following Jesus as "the Truth," speaking truth, and living forever with God? Or getting some cheap, quick advantage by lying?

Lord God, please make me strong in the truth—Your truth. I want to honor You with my honesty.

HELP ALL

They gave clothing to all of them who had none, using the clothes found among the things taken from Judah. They gave them clothes and shoes, and food and drink, and poured oil on them. They led all their weak ones on donkeys, and brought them to their brothers at Jericho, the city of palm trees. Then they returned to Samaria.
2 Chronicles 28:15

A little history lesson will help you understand this verse. In the Old Testament, God's people were called *Israel*. They became a nation with kings like David and Solomon, but when Solomon died, his foolish son Rehoboam made a lot of people mad. So the northern people split from the south, creating two nations—Israel and Judah.

They were all Jews, but they often fought. In 2 Chronicles, Israel's army had just defeated Judah's soldiers in battle. And Israel wanted to make them slaves.

But a prophet told Israel that would make God angry. So Israel changed direction and *helped* Judah's soldiers with food, clothing, and medical care.

If God wants us to help even our enemies, shouldn't we be eager to help our friends and family?

Lord, please give me a heart for helping.

GOD LOVES YOU

"I say to you, My friends, do not be afraid of those who kill the body and then can do no more."
LUKE 12:4

Watching the news can be frightening. Lots of bad things happen every day. Sometimes people get hurt. Sometimes they get killed. That's a good reason to pray, but it's not a good reason to be afraid.

You may not realize it yet, but the time you'll live in this world is pretty short. Someday, though, Christians will live with God forever. Death doesn't stop that from happening. *It can't.*

If you follow Him, Jesus promised to make a home for you in heaven. No one—not popular, angry, or mean people—can take that away. The worst they can do is make life unpleasant here. But when you die, there will be a welcome home party for you in heaven.

Maybe this isn't the easiest thing to think about, but it means that *God loves you*. He cares about you. He looks forward to showing you the home He made for you.

And it's going to be awesome.

Lord, thank You for making a perfect place where I can be with You forever.

TESTING GOD

"Bring the tenth part into the store-house, so that there may be food in My house. Test Me in this," says the Lord of All. "See if I will not then open the windows of heaven and pour out good things for you until there is no more need."

MALACHI 3:10

It might sound scary to "test God." But in today's verse, God tells His people to do just that by their giving. If His people *will* test Him, God promises to meet their needs.

Back in the book of Nehemiah (chapter 13), we see that God's people had not given all they should have. The house of God—kind of like our churches today—wasn't being cared for. Church workers had even been forced to take other jobs. In Malachi, God told the people to give so that His house would be cared for—and then He promised to give back to them, pouring out good things.

When you put money in the collection plate, it helps support the work of the church. Be brave and generous—and watch for the good things God will do!

Father God, may I "test You" by being generous with my money.

BOLD LIKE SAMUEL

Now Samuel was serving the Lord, even as a boy.
1 Samuel 2:18

As a grown-up, Samuel did a lot of important things. He guided the nation of Israel as they chose a king. He told people whatever God told him to say, even when they didn't want to hear it. Samuel worked hard for God—but that started long before he was a man.

Even as a boy, Samuel served the Lord. From the time he was born, he was set apart to be God's servant. He grew up in the temple and was raised by the head priest, Eli.

Although Eli loved God, his sons did not. They stole from people and took offerings that were supposed to be for God. Even though people were making bad choices around Samuel, he still followed the Lord. While others ignored God, Samuel listened to Him.

When you are surrounded by people doing bad things, you still have the choice to do what God tells you. Be bold like Samuel and choose to listen to God. You can do important things for Him too!

Lord, help me to make good choices even when people around me don't.

WALKING ON WATER!

At once Jesus spoke to them and said,
"Take hope. It is I. Do not be afraid!"
MATTHEW 14:27

You've probably heard how Jesus once walked on water. That's a miracle! Unless it's frozen, nobody else can walk on water.

Well, nobody except the apostle Peter. He was on a boat with the other disciples when Jesus came walking toward them—on the water, in the dark, during a crazy storm. It was such a strange scene that the disciples actually thought Jesus was a ghost. But He said, "It is I. Do not be afraid!"

That's when Peter said, "If it is You, Lord, tell me to come to You on the water." Jesus said, "Come," and Peter too started walking on the water!

But soon Peter got distracted. As soon as he stopped looking at Jesus—paying more attention to the storm—he sank. Happily, Jesus grabbed Peter's hand and saved him.

When you're in a scary situation, be sure to keep your eyes on Jesus. He will see you through every one of life's storms.

God, please give me Peter's boldness to come to You—but don't let me get distracted by the storm.

DAY 138

CONNECTED TO GOD

"Look to the Lord and ask for His strength. Look to Him all the time."
1 Chronicles 16:11

How many things in your house run on electricity? You'd probably be surprised to add them up—refrigerators, toasters, computers, garage-door openers, lamps, TVs—the list is long. One thing they all have in common is that they need to be plugged in to a power source. If the cord is just lying loose on the floor, that device won't do anything but sit there.

That's kind of a picture of prayer. It is our connection to God, a way of plugging in to our "power source." God wants us to be strong in His strength, and the main way we do that is to pray to Him often. We can pray over a test at school, for a sick loved one, or even if we're afraid of the dark.

Jesus told His disciples, "Let the little children come to Me" (Mark 10:14), so you know He wants to hear from you. Go ahead—whatever is bothering you right now, speak up. Your heavenly Father is always listening.

Father, I thank You for Your power. Please help me to stay connected.

WHAT ALWAYS COMES TRUE

Every good promise which the Lord had made to the people of Israel came true.
JOSHUA 21:45

When you were younger, were you ever told anything that wasn't true? Easter bunny, anyone? Tooth fairy? *Oh yeah, and a whole lot more.*

When Ben was little, a schoolteacher told a story about wishing on a flower to make things come true. So when it was time for Ben's favorite cousin to drive away, he quickly ran across the yard, picked a flower, and wished for his cousin to stay "forever." Of course, a few minutes later, Ben's cousin disappeared down the road.

Later his dad explained that wishes on flowers—or over birthday candles or when you're tossing a coin into a well—are made just for fun. They don't always come true. What always comes true? Only God's promises in the Bible.

Lord, wishes are fun, but Your promises are forever. Thank You for the wonderful promise of new, eternal life. I believe Jesus died on the cross for my sins. I believe He rose from the dead on the third day. I want to receive Him as my Lord and Savior.

STICK TO THE BIBLE

"Do not add to the Word that I tell you, and do not take away from it. Keep the Laws of the Lord your God which I tell you."
DEUTERONOMY 4:2

People love new stuff. That's why car companies, phone makers, video game designers, and movie producers are always advertising "the latest and greatest." They make a lot of money from people who have to have new things.

But here's one thing you should never replace with something new: the Bible. God gave us His Word so we could know Him and what He wants for us. And since God never changes, His Word doesn't change either. As Jesus' friend and follower, Peter wrote, "The Word of the Lord will last forever" (1 Peter 1:25).

Some people don't like what the Bible says, so they try to change it. They add their own thoughts to it. Or they take away parts of the Bible they don't like. Or they just ignore God's rules entirely. Brave boys, though, obey God's Word—every part of it.

Stick to the Bible, and God will stick with you.

Lord God, please give me the courage to stand with Your Word.

KEEPING THE RULE BOOK

You obey the whole Law when you do this one thing, "Love your neighbor as you love yourself."
GALATIANS 5:14

Someone once asked Jesus to explain the word *neighbor*. To do so, He told a story.

Jesus described a man who was hurt on the side of the road. Two men who had studied God's rules saw the man but walked by without helping him. They knew better than that. But then a man from another country came by. He stopped, helped the injured man, and made sure he was taken care of.

Jesus' point was that your "neighbor" is really anyone you meet. So when God says to "love your neighbor," He means you should love *everyone*. Even those guys who could have helped out but didn't.

When you truly care about people—when you stop to listen, offer help, pray, and encourage others—God says you're obeying His entire Law. That's how you keep the rule book for life.

Heavenly Father, You loved me and made me Your child. Because of Your love, I can love You back—now help me to love others too.

TOMORROW ISN'T CERTAIN

Do not talk much about tomorrow,
for you do not know what a day will bring.
Proverbs 27:1

Some people (usually older ones) think a lot about the way things used to be. Other people (usually younger ones) think a lot about tomorrow. But the scriptures tell us not to think too much about either. We can't do anything about the past, and the future isn't in our hands. What we can control are our actions in this minute.

It's so easy to waste time. Video games, YouTube, being lazy. . .sometimes we act as if we have all the time in the world, but we don't really know that. James 4:13–14 says, "Listen! You who say, 'Today or tomorrow we will go to this city and stay a year and make money.' You do not know about tomorrow. What is your life? It is like fog. You see it and soon it is gone."

Brave boys use their time wisely, even when other guys are just fooling around. Set a good example for them—maybe even for the adults around you.

Father, help me to make good decisions on how I spend my time.

BECAUSE HE CARES

The Lord punishes everyone He loves.
PROVERBS 3:12

In some Bible translations, the word *punishes* in Proverbs 3:12 is "disciplines." As your heavenly Father, God does what good earthly fathers do—He punishes or disciplines His children when they need it. This is done out of the deepest love, because God cares about His creation. Through discipline, God keeps you from danger.

Think about it this way: Let's say you're not allowed to go to a friend's house when their parents are gone, but you disobey and go anyway. You'll probably get grounded, right? That's because parents know it's not safe for kids to be unsupervised. Your parents will *discipline* you because they love you.

God does the same thing. Even though Jesus took the punishment for our sins when He died on the cross, we still need to be reminded to do the right thing. We still make mistakes, and when we do, God will be faithful to remind us of what's right. When He disciplines, it's because He cares.

Lord God, You are holy. I thank You for loving me enough to discipline me. May Your Word make me a better, braver boy.

FOLLOW PAUL'S EXAMPLE

Follow my way of thinking as I follow Christ.
1 Corinthians 11:1

When the apostle Paul says, "Follow my way of thinking," he's inviting you to think, choose, live, and love like he did. Basically, he's saying: "Think about Jesus like I do. Choose to obey Jesus like I do. Live for Jesus like I do. Love others because you love Jesus like I do. Follow my example just as I follow Jesus Christ's example, each and every day."

So how do you do that? Well, you've already made a good start. You're reading these devotions. You're thinking about the Bible verses that go with them. You're praying the prayers. Don't stop now! Take your time with every devotional—one page a day, read slowly and thoughtfully with a heartfelt prayer at the end.

Read the verse above once again. Then read these paragraphs again. Then pray the prayer below with gusto. It's going to be a great day!

Lord, I thank You for these devotions, which are based on Your Word. I'm so glad they're helping me learn how to follow Jesus Christ better and better.

DAY 145

THE GIFT OF STRENGTH

I want to see you so I can share some special gift of the Holy Spirit with you. It will make you strong.
ROMANS 1:11

You don't have to be naturally courageous to be a brave boy. You just need to allow God's Holy Spirit to work in your life.

The apostle Paul admitted that he wasn't an impressive guy. He once wrote down what other people said about him: "When he is here with us, he is weak and he is hard to listen to" (2 Corinthians 10:10). But you'd have a hard time finding a more courageous man in all of history. He preached the good news about Jesus no matter how many times he was arrested, thrown in jail, beaten, stoned, and shipwrecked. How could he do that?

Only by the gift of the Holy Spirit, which made him (and will make *us*) strong.

If you're not super brave, super brainy, or super brawny, that's okay. God will be happy to *give* you whatever power you need to serve Him. Just ask. Then move forward in His strength.

Father, I want the power of Your Holy Spirit. Please make me strong to do Your work.

DAY 146

THE THINGS YOU NEED

"Do not worry. Do not keep saying, 'What will we eat?' or, 'What will we drink?' or, 'What will we wear?' The people who do not know God are looking for all these things. Your Father in heaven knows you need all these things."

MATTHEW 6:31–32

When you're hungry, thirsty, or wondering where you put your favorite shirt, you need to remember this: While so many other people worry about things, God doesn't. He knows what you need. And He wants you to know that there's nothing you worry about that He can't handle.

You probably think about food at least three times a day. (Some boys never stop thinking about food!) You get thirsty several times a day. God made the things you eat and the water you drink. He made the raw materials for the clothes you wear and the wood and stone that make up the house you live in. He knows what you need, and He provides it. Don't worry!

Father, when I sit down to dinner, drink a bottle of water, or slide a shirt over my head, please help me to worry less and thank You more.

JOSEPH'S REVENGE

"So do not be afraid. I will take care of you and your little ones." He gave them comfort and words of kindness.

GENESIS 50:21

You probably know the story of Joseph and his coat of many colors. Joseph's jealous brothers hated the fact that their dad liked Joseph best, so they sold him into slavery and told their dad that Joseph had died.

Many years later, Joseph was reunited with his father and provided food for his starving brothers. But when their father died, the brothers worried that Joseph would want revenge.

Instead of getting back at his brothers, though, Joseph gave them comfort. He promised good things to them with kind words. Though no one would have blamed Joseph for treating his brothers badly, he chose to be kind.

When someone treats you wrong, it's tempting to want revenge. But when you offer forgiveness instead, you not only follow in Joseph's steps—you follow in Jesus' steps as well. That's the brave way to go.

Lord, help me to forgive when I feel like getting revenge. May others see my example and know it is because You have forgiven me.

THE JOY OF GOD'S POWER

Let the joy of Your saving power return to me.
And give me a willing spirit to obey you.
Psalm 51:12

David wrote Psalm 51 after committing a huge sin. He realized that he'd messed up, and he didn't make any excuses to God. Instead, David said his sin was always in front of him. He couldn't forget it! So he asked God to wash him inside and out for his wrongdoing. David missed the closeness he'd felt with God in the past, and he wanted God to return his joy.

The loss of joy happens when we sin—especially when we commit the same sin over and over without asking God's forgiveness. We begin to feel separated from Him and powerless to turn away from wrong. We really *are* powerless when we choose to walk away from God. But He's always calling us to return to Him.

If you're feeling far away from God, ask yourself if it's because of sin. If that's true, make Psalm 51 your prayer today. The joy of God's saving power will return to you.

Lord, forgive me for my sin.
And give me a willing spirit to obey You.

SURROUNDED

Many are the sorrows of the sinful. But loving-kindness will be all around the man who trusts in the Lord.
Psalm 32:10

Imagine that you're a soldier in battle. Do you want to be surrounded?

It depends. You certainly don't want to be surrounded by the enemy. But if you're surrounded by your own fellow soldiers, and they're well armed and well trained, that's a different story.

Psalm 32:10 pictures both situations. Sinful people are surrounded by many sorrows—since they don't obey God, they bring a lot of trouble to themselves. But "the man who trusts in the Lord" is surrounded by "loving-kindness"—that's God's loving-kindness—all the good things He promises to those who follow Jesus. Things like love, joy, peace, kindness, goodness. . .and, in the end, eternal life.

God is always watching over you. When you trust Him—when you believe in who He is and what He says, when you know and obey His Word—loving-kindness will be all around you. That's a great way to be surrounded!

Lord God, this life is a battle. Please surround me with Your goodness and protection.

YOU JUST DON'T KNOW

Do not be ashamed to tell others about what our Lord said, or of me here in prison. I am here because of Jesus Christ. Be ready to suffer for preaching the Good News and God will give you the strength you need.
2 Timothy 1:8

Do you know what a martyr is? It's a person who gives his or her life in exchange for their beliefs. In the Bible, Stephen was one of the first Christian martyrs (Acts 7). He was not afraid to share God's Word, no matter the cost.

Can you imagine that? Being more concerned with telling about Jesus than keeping your own life? What a brave example!

In Acts 8 we see that someone was watching Stephen—an angry religious leader named Saul. Before long, Jesus Himself would appear to Saul, telling him to become a great preacher of the gospel. Saul's name would be changed to Paul, and he turned into one of the most important leaders of the early church.

Do you think Stephen's example might have had an influence on the change in Saul? What influence might *your* example have on someone?

Father, help me to boldly share my faith today.

DAY 151

FORGIVING SOMEONE OVER AND OVER

"What if he sins against you seven times in one day? If he comes to you and says he is sorry and turns from his sin, forgive him."
LUKE 17:4

Zach was excited to get an adopted sister. At first, he had a lot of fun playing with her. But one day she bit Zach on the arm. He scolded her, but she did it again the next day. And the next. "Mom," Zach asked, "what am I going to do?"

His mom explained that Zach needed to forgive his new sister. "She won't keep biting you forever," Mom said. "But right now she's scared. And sometimes when she feels scared, she bites. It hurts—I know. We just have to hang in there, ask her to say she's sorry, and keep forgiving her."

Many people think this teaching of Jesus is crazy, but He knows what He's talking about. Ask Him for bravery to do something that many people won't—forgive others, over and over. God will make sure it all works out.

Lord, I'm glad You always forgive me. But it's sometimes hard for me to forgive. Give me the courage to trust and obey You.

NO PRIDE ALLOWED

I can only speak of what Christ has done through me.
Romans 15:18

In the 1800s, a man named George Müller believed God wanted him to care for English orphans. Orphans are children whose mothers and fathers have died. Müller prayed that God would give him money and food to care for many of these needy kids.

God answered those prayers. Over sixty years, this one man fed, clothed, and housed more than *ten thousand* orphans! He also gave away hundreds of thousands of Bibles.

Isn't that impressive? Yes, but. . .

George Müller would say it wasn't because of him. "No one should admire me, be astonished at my faith, or think of me as if I were an amazing person," he wrote. Like the apostle Paul in Romans 15:18, George Müller could "only speak of what Christ has done through me."

A lot of things have changed since the 1800s, but human pride hasn't. So many people say, "Look at me! Look at what I've done!" Brave boys and men say, "Look at God! Look at what He does!"

Father, help me to squash my pride and boldly tell what Jesus has done.

DON'T WORRY, FOLLOW JESUS

"Only a few things are important, even just one. Mary has chosen the good thing. It will not be taken away from her."
LUKE 10:42

If you have a brother or sister or a good friend you've spent much time with, you've probably seen them make choices that are different than ones you would make. Many choices aren't that important, but some are better than others.

Jesus was a friend to two sisters, Mary and Martha. Martha wanted everything to be perfect—she cared a lot about what other people thought of her work. But Mary was more interested in learning from Jesus. While Martha worked hard on dinner, Mary sat and listened to Jesus. Martha got upset.

But Jesus told Martha that she worried too much. He said that Mary had made a good choice.

You'll probably have times when you worry about what other people think. But don't be like Martha. . .pray for the courage to be like Mary. Just follow Jesus.

Lord, please help me to care most about what You think. When I care more about other people's opinions, I might stop following where You lead.

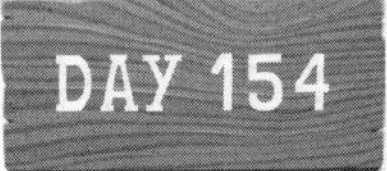

DON'T BE FOOLISH

"The fields of a rich man gave much grain. The rich man thought to himself, 'What will I do? I have no place to put the grain.' Then he said, 'I know what I will do. I will take down my grain building and I will build a bigger one. I will put all my grain and other things I own into it. And I will say to my soul, "Soul, you have many good things put away in your building. It will be all you need for many years to come. Now rest and eat and drink and have lots of fun."'"

Luke 12:16–19

The rich man's plans sound good, don't they? He had too much grain for his barn, so why not build a bigger one? Well, the next couple of verses explain why.

Turns out the man was going to die that night. He'd spent so much time storing things for his future that he hadn't spent time investing in God's kingdom. This man's problem wasn't storing grain; it was missing out on living for God.

Let's be sure we don't make the same mistake.

Lord, help me to invest in Your kingdom.

BE LIKE NOAH

Noah did just what God told him to do.
GENESIS 6:22

One great thing about being obedient is knowing that God is always with you—no matter what. He is there to help you, to guide you, and to remind you to ask for forgiveness when you mess up.

Noah obeyed God in a huge way. The Bible says that the world was a very bad place during Noah's lifetime because nobody else wanted to obey God. So the Lord decided to send a flood to wash the world clean. Noah, though, was going to be saved along with his family.

As hard as it was to imagine, Noah believed that God would do as He said. And for the next hundred years, he and his family built the ark. God saved them—and two of every kind of animal—from the great flood.

When we obey the directions He has for us, God gives us daily comfort. Stick with Him! Don't quit. Be patient and watch how God will take your life to awesome places.

Lord God, please help me to listen to Your Word. Then give me the strength to obey!

DAY 156

WORK WHILE YOU WAIT

"I know what you have done and how hard you have worked. I know how long you can wait and not give up."
REVELATION 2:2

God gave Noah instructions for building that massive boat called the ark. Then Noah was to bring two of every animal into the ark with him and wait for the rains to fall.

That ark was huge—as long as one and a half football fields! We don't know if Noah and his three sons built it all by themselves, or if they hired other people to help. But it must have taken a long time. You can imagine the sinful people around them laughing as they worked on their strange project. But then, just like God had said, the whole earth flooded. Only Noah and his family were saved.

Noah waited patiently for God's promise, but he also waited *actively*—he did the job God gave him to do. And so should we. As we wait for Jesus to return to earth, we must tell other people about His salvation. Like Noah, let's be both patient and brave.

Lord God, please help me to work while I wait. . .for Jesus!

PUT GOD FIRST

Elijah said to her, "Have no fear. Go and do as you have said. But make me a little loaf of bread from it first, and bring it out to me. Then you may make one for yourself and for your son."

1 Kings 17:13

Here's an interesting story: The prophet Elijah needed food, and God told him to ask a poor widow for help. She was preparing to bake with her last bit of flour. When Elijah asked for food, she said that she and her son were going to eat their little loaf of bread. . .and die.

Do you think God forgot how poor this lady was?

Hardly. He was going to perform a miracle.

Elijah told the woman to bake, but to give the loaf to *him*. Then, when she returned to her flour and oil containers, they wouldn't be empty—there would always be more for her to use. That's exactly what happened!

Why did things work out so well? Because this lady did what God said. She listened to Elijah, obeyed his word, and was blessed by God.

God always blesses those who put Him first.

**Lord, may I always put You first—
and enjoy Your blessing.**

LAUGHING AT JESUS

Jesus heard it and said to Jairus, "Do not be afraid, only believe. She will be made well."
LUKE 8:50

Even Jesus got laughed at sometimes.

After performing amazing miracles—like casting out demons and controlling the weather—Jesus was welcomed to Jairus's town by people who knew He had power. Jairus begged Jesus to heal his dying daughter, but while Jesus was healing someone else, the twelve-year-old died.

Everyone believed Jesus could heal the sick, but when He said the dead girl was only "sleeping," people laughed at Him. They thought Jesus wasn't smart enough to recognize death—or surely not powerful enough to overcome it. But while they laughed, Jesus brought the girl back to life.

Sometimes, people will laugh at your belief in God. They might think you aren't smart or that God isn't powerful—but Jesus has dealt with all that stuff before. Let people laugh, knowing that Jesus has raised you up to eternal life with Him. Maybe, at some point, they'll wise up and believe in Jesus too.

Lord, help me to be bold even when people laugh at my belief in You.

A TIME TO TAKE CARE

Anyone who does not take care of his family and those in his house has turned away from the faith. He is worse than a person who has never put his trust in Christ.
1 TIMOTHY 5:8

God never asks you to do something He doesn't do. He wouldn't ask you to forgive if He never forgave. He wouldn't ask you to love others if He didn't love you. He wouldn't ask you to be kind if He was rude.

These are the attitudes and behaviors He wants you to have in your family.

Family is important. So important that the Bible tells us to take care of each member.

Some families are happy and strong. Others need help. But God is there for every kind of family and every boy in them.

God is a Father who looks after the needs of His family. If you have a happy home, thank Him for that and make sure you serve everyone well. If your home has problems, pray for God's help. And ask Him to make you forgiving, loving, and kind. . .like Jesus.

Father, You forgive, love, and show kindness. Help me do that for my family.

WORKING TOGETHER

Two are better than one,
because they have good pay for their work.
ECCLESIASTES 4:9

Did you ever watch the show *Thomas & Friends*? If so, maybe you've seen an episode titled "Two Hooks Are Better Than One." In that story, Kevin, a small crane, is convinced that Cranky, a much larger crane, doesn't like him. When Cranky struggles with a job, Kevin jumps in to help. But Kevin ends up falling into the water, and Cranky has to save him. Once everyone is safe, they realize they should work together because "two hooks are better than one."

When you do chores with a brother or sister, or when you help a friend with a project, you might not always see eye to eye. But you both want to get the job done right. The sooner you understand this, the sooner you can accomplish more by working together.

That's what King Solomon was saying in today's Bible verse. God wants you to work with others to achieve your tasks and goals. It's not always easy, but it's definitely worth it in the end.

Lord, please help me to work well with others and to do great things for You.

RUN TO JESUS

Let us put every thing out of our lives that keeps us from doing what we should. Let us keep running in the race that God has planned for us. Let us keep looking to Jesus.
Hebrews 12:1–2

Pretend you are standing in a huge stadium, waiting on the track to run a very long race. The stands are packed with people who love Jesus like you do. And they are all there to cheer you on! The Bible's book of Hebrews paints this picture to help you, as God's child, understand that you are not alone.

Now imagine that you're looking at the finish line—there's Jesus! He is the goal and the prize of this race. Keep your eyes on Him as you run, and don't get distracted by anything else. Jesus ran this race before you did, and He will help you to finish.

What tough things are you dealing with right now? Jesus can handle them. He will help you overcome the struggles because He is faithful. Look to Jesus! Run to Him!

God, sometimes I don't feel strong at all. Please remind me to "run to Jesus" in prayer.

BE TRUSTWORTHY

They did not ask the men who paid those who did the work how the money was spent. For they were men of honor.
2 Kings 12:15

Here's an interesting fact about the Bible character Joash: He became king when he was seven years old!

When he was thirty, Joash started a big repair job on God's temple in Jerusalem. The priest Jehoiada, who had guided Joash through his boyhood as king, set up an offering box at the temple. People gave lots of money, and a group of workers stepped in to hire carpenters, masons, stonecutters, and other people who made the actual repairs. The king and the priest trusted those workers so much that they never asked how they were spending the money. The Bible says, "They were men of honor."

Even today God wants men (and boys!) of honor. It takes time to develop that kind of reputation, but it's worth it. When you say you'll do something, do it. When someone trusts you with something valuable, take care of it. When you have a chance to do the wrong thing, do the right thing instead!

Heavenly Father, please help me to be trustworthy.

THE BEST FOOD IN THE WORLD

Jesus said, "My food is to do what God wants Me to do and to finish His work."
JOHN 4:34

Leon played soccer with some guys who were really good. "The Sharks" were so good that they usually won their games by scores like 5–0, 8–0, even 11–0. As a defender, Leon rarely ran around, let alone touched the ball.

One day, Leon's dad took him to the field an hour before the game. He helped Leon picture himself stealing the ball and making good passes. He also taught Leon to yell "Shark attack!" as soon as the whistle blew. Suddenly, playing soccer was much more exciting. And after the game, snacks were the last thing on Leon's mind. Instead, he ran over to do a fist bump with his dad.

It's kind of like that when you do what God wants you to do—you feel *energized*. The experience is even better than your favorite lunch. Today, ask your dad or mom to help you picture yourself doing something God wants you to do.

Lord, I want to love doing what You want me to do. That sounds like the best "food" in the world.

DAY 164

FOR YOU, IS JESUS CHRIST #1?

Christ is the head of the church which is His body. He is the beginning of all things. He is the first to be raised from the dead. He is to have first place in everything.

COLOSSIANS 1:18

The question in the title above is important. So is the Bible verse, which ends by saying Jesus "is to have first place in everything." And, yes, "everything" means *every single thing* in your heart and life.

Today, millions of grown-ups—in this country and around the world—have some pretty mistaken ideas. They believe that "reality is all in your mind." They think, *I can pick and choose whatever I want to believe.* That kind of thinking is foolishness. . .it doesn't work. Reality doesn't have any exceptions. The facts are the facts. And the #1 fact in the universe is this: Jesus "is to have first place in everything."

For you, today, is Jesus Christ #11? Or maybe #8? Or is He #1?

It's your choice. The fact that you're reading this devotional book is a good sign. Now pray and make sure.

Lord, right now, in my heart and life, I want to make Jesus Christ #1.

SCOLDED

Strong words that punish are the way of life.
PROVERBS 6:23

Who enjoys being scolded? Not many of us. But the Bible says correction and instruction—"strong words that punish"—are the way of life.

That means spiritual life, the kind that goes on long after our bodies get old and die. To find "life that lasts forever" (John 3:16), we need to hear some strong words first. Words like "all men have sinned and have missed the shining-greatness of God" (Romans 3:23). Or, "You get what is coming to you when you sin. It is death!" (Romans 6:23).

When we learn how much our sin upsets God, we can deal with it. And we can only deal with sin God's way—by believing that Jesus died on the cross to take our punishment, then rose again to show His power. That's why the second half of Romans 6:23 says, "God's free gift is life that lasts forever. It is given to us by our Lord Jesus Christ."

Being scolded isn't fun. But "strong words that punish are the way of life."

Lord God, I thank You for loving me enough to speak strong words that lead to life.

INTRODUCTIONS

The Lord showed Himself to Isaac that same night, and said, "I am the God of your father Abraham. Do not be afraid, for I am with you."
GENESIS 26:24

Once in a while, someone you don't know will walk up and say your name—maybe even shake your hand. It seems strange, and it might make you a little fearful. Usually, though, you'll find that the person is a family member you've never met or a friend of your parents. When Mom or Dad helps you understand how the person knows you, the fear goes away.

In the Bible, God introduced Himself to Isaac and told him not to be afraid. That's because this was the same God who knew Isaac's father. This was the God who had helped his family. This was the God who had made promises and kept them. Now God promised to be with Isaac too.

God is with you as well. He doesn't want you to be afraid. He wants to share some pretty great plans for your life.

Father, I want to know You. I want to be Your friend. Help me not to be frightened but to learn more about You.

GIVE—AND GET?

"Give, and it will be given to you. You will have more than enough. It can be pushed down and shaken together and it will still run over as it is given to you. The way you give to others is the way you will receive in return."
Luke 6:38

Armando Beltran spent most of his childhood in foster care. He rode his bike several miles to school, and he even lived in a shack for a while. But that didn't stop him from volunteering at the school library and helping the staff whenever they needed something.

When Armando was a nineteen-year-old senior, one of his teachers nominated him for a program called "Pay It 4Ward." And he won an award worth four hundred dollars! Armando didn't expect to get anything for his volunteering, but when he did, he was grateful. It helped him pay some bills.

God tells His children that being generous does have rewards. We shouldn't give just to get something back, but God promises that our generous giving will come around to help us. That's quite a deal!

Lord, please help me to be generous. I can never give more than You do!

TELL THEM ABOUT JESUS

The next night the Lord came to Paul and said, "Paul, do not be afraid! You will tell about Me in the city of Rome the same as you have told about Me in Jerusalem."
ACTS 23:11

Being brave is deciding to live for God. That's what the apostle Paul did with his life. He went from place to place and told people about Jesus. He was very careful to tell the truth clearly, making sure that everyone knew Jesus had died for their sins and that there was no way to God the Father except through Jesus.

Many people didn't like what Paul was saying. But he didn't let that stop him from sharing the good news of the gospel. Jesus told Paul not to be afraid of anything, because God would protect him. And God helped Paul to finish the work he was called to do.

So, how about you? Are you choosing to live each day for Jesus? Be brave, and remember that He is always there to help you!

Lord, I thank You for Paul's story. Help me to be like him and tell my friends that Jesus loves them.

JONAH'S PROMISE

"But I will give gifts in worship to You with a thankful voice. I will give You what I have promised. The Lord is the One Who saves."
Jonah 2:9

The prophet Jonah once made a big promise to the Lord. At the time, he was in the belly of an enormous fish!

Hard as it may be to believe, Jonah had been there for three days. He thought he was going to die, so he made a commitment to God. Part of his promise was to praise and worship the Lord with thanksgiving.

Before long, the fish belched Jonah onto the beach. He must have looked (and smelled) terrible. Still, he went to Nineveh to preach, as God had said. Though he was obeying, he wasn't happy about it. So much for that "with a thankful voice" thing.

Jonah's story ends with him angry and wanting to die. Was that just because he made a promise he didn't keep? Well, it certainly didn't help anything!

Lord, if I ever make a promise to You, help me to keep 100 percent of it.

RESPECTING GIRLS

The shepherds came and tried to make [the women] go away. But Moses stood up and helped them. He gave water to their flock.

Exodus 2:17

It's sad to realize that many men have mistreated women. And that's been going on for a long, long time.

But many other men, for a long, long time, have respected girls. Moses was one of them.

After Moses left Egypt, he ended up in a place called Midian. As he arrived at a well, he watched some local shepherds mistreating the priest's daughters. Moses decided to step in.

If it hasn't happened yet, someday you'll realize that you like girls. Defending them against people who treat them poorly, combined with helping them in their work, is a great way to get their attention. But even if you're not "looking for a girlfriend," remember that every girl is worthy of respect and kindness. They bear God's image every bit as much as guys do.

Today, think about how you could defend girls against unfairness. How can you properly honor them?

Lord, You made girls to be amazing because you made them in Your own image. Help me to treat them with kindness and respect.

JUST ASK!

"Ask, and what you are asking for will be given to you. Look, and what you are looking for you will find. Knock, and the door you are knocking on will be opened to you."
MATTHEW 7:7

Have you ever started to pray about something then wondered if you should? Maybe it was a small, simple request like help for a homework problem. Or maybe it was a huge, seemingly impossible request like healing for someone with cancer.

When you have a need, Jesus says to ask, look, and knock. Take the request to God. Watch for His answer. If it's taking a while, keep knocking on His door. Jesus said the Father *wants* to help you: "What man among you would give his son a stone if he should ask for bread? Or if he asks for a fish, would he give him a snake? You are bad and you know how to give good things to your children. How much more will your Father in heaven give good things to those who ask Him?" (Matthew 7:9–11).

Whatever your need, big or small, go to God. Just ask!

Father, please help me to bring every request to You.

DAY 172

PLAY THE RIGHT NOTES

I may be able to speak the languages of men and even of angels, but if I do not have love, it will sound like noisy brass. If I have the gift of speaking God's Word and if I understand all secrets, but do not have love, I am nothing. If I know all things and if I have the gift of faith so I can move mountains, but do not have love, I am nothing.

1 Corinthians 13:1–2

Try saying, "I believe in God, but I'm too busy to care about you." Did that sound wrong?

How about this? "I have memorized a dozen verses from the Bible, and that makes me better than you."

When you don't speak in love, you sound like a band that can't play the right notes. You seem rude, unkind, and stuck up. That's a song no one wants to hear.

But love changes everything. Kindness, humility, and caring are the right notes. God—and everyone around you—will be pleased.

Father, love is never too busy for others. It doesn't put people down. It's kind, shares, and hangs in there when things get tough. Help me do that.

NOBODY KNOWS

No man knows what will happen.
And who can tell him what will come after him?
Ecclesiastes 10:14

Have you ever been around someone who thinks he knows who's going to win the Super Bowl or the NBA championship? Or maybe he claims to know exactly what's going to be on the next math test. He talks and talks, acting like his opinion is reality—and even if he ends up wrong, he still thinks he's right.

Ecclesiastes 10:13 says that kind of talk starts out foolish—in the end, it's sinful and crazy. No human being knows exactly what will happen in the future, so don't ever pretend that you do. Stick to the truths the Bible makes clear—like the fact that Jesus is in heaven, preparing a place for His followers, and that He will definitely return to earth someday. But don't go beyond what scripture says.

Be humble in your conversations with people. Don't brag or act like you know everything. When you speak carefully, God will be pleased. And others might even want to know more about Him.

Lord, help me to think before I speak.
I never want to speak foolishly.

FINDING YOUR WAY

Before I suffered I went the wrong way,
but now I obey Your Word.
Psalm 119:67

The Bible is like a road map. It tells how to find your ultimate destination—God. But if you don't read your Bible, you'll just get lost in the chaos of the world.

When you find yourself in tough times, open your Bible. If it says you've done something wrong, you will feel conviction. That's not a bad thing—let God use that conviction to guide you back onto His path.

That's what the psalm writer did. He said that he was going the wrong way and suffered for it, but God's Word showed him where he went wrong. But when he chose to obey God's Word, life was good again. In fact, just a few verses later, he said that God's Word was "better to me than thousands of gold and silver pieces" (verse 72).

Don't be afraid of suffering and conviction. They have a way of leading us back to God.

Thank You, God, for loving me.
Help me to stay connected to You.
When I wander, lead me back to You.

DAY 175

EYES TO YOURSELF

Each has his own gift from God.
One has one gift. Another has another gift.
1 CORINTHIANS 7:7

When they hand out test papers, teachers say things like "Keep your eyes to yourself." They don't want you looking at someone else's work.

Today's verse says something similar about the Christian life. The apostle Paul was writing about spiritual gifts, the talents and abilities that God gives each person who receives Jesus. These gifts are supposed to be used to help other Christians.

That's all good—unless we get our eyes off ourselves. Sometimes people look at other people's gifts and feel envious. They wish they could preach or teach or sing in front of people too.

But every gift is needed, and God gives different gifts to everyone. If you're more of a behind-the-scenes guy, that's great. Be a helper, an encourager, or even the guy who volunteers to clean the church. Not everyone will notice you, but the most important person—Jesus—will.

Lord, thank You for giving me my own gifts. Please help me to use them every day to accomplish great things for You.

DAY 176

JEHOSHA-WHO?

The Lord was with Jehoshaphat because he followed the early ways of his father. He did not follow the false gods of Baal.
2 CHRONICLES 17:3

Have you ever heard someone shout, "Jumping Jehoshaphat!"? People said that a lot back in the 1900s. Many said it even though they didn't know who Jehoshaphat was. If you need to know, he was one of the good kings of Judah. He lived many years after King David.

While Jehoshaphat was growing up, his dad was king. Asa was good for many years, but then he rebelled against the Lord—and never repented. That means he never turned away from his sinful ways. He never turned back to God.

Did Jehoshaphat grow up and do the same thing? Thankfully, no. Well, Jehoshaphat *did* sin, but he always was sorry about that and turned back to God wholeheartedly.

Does God expect you to be perfect? That would be ideal, but God knows you're going to sin sometimes. You're going to have moments when you disobey. The question is this: Are you going to admit your sin and turn back to God?

Lord, You know my sin. I'm sorry. Thank You for always forgiving me.

YES, I WOULD

Jesus saw him lying there and knew the man had been sick a long time. Jesus said to him, "Would you like to be healed?"
JOHN 5:6

Ever heard the word *killjoy*? It describes someone who spoils other people's pleasure. Sadly, many people think God is a killjoy—that He's up in heaven, looking for opportunities to take away our happiness. But that's far from the truth.

Jesus—God in a human body—constantly helped others. Over and over, the Bible shows Him casting demons from people, giving sight to the blind, and helping the paralyzed to walk. In John 5:6, Jesus asked a man who'd been sick a long time (*thirty-eight years!*), "Would you like to be healed?" Then He performed a miracle that allowed the man to get up and walk away. That doesn't sound like a killjoy!

Would you like the God of the whole universe to help *you*? Would you like Him to give you wisdom, peace, happiness, or bravery? If your answer is "Yes, I would," then ask Him. He's in the business of *adding* joy to people's lives.

Yes, Father, I would like every blessing You'll give me. Thank You!

DAY 178

WORRY'S DISTRACTIONS

When my worry is great within me,
Your comfort brings joy to my soul.
Psalm 94:19

When you're home alone, being bullied at school, or have a test over material you don't understand, you can worry. When confusing things happen, you can become anxious. Those troublesome thoughts can take over your life, pushing the truth from your mind. God knows that's never a good place for His children to be. He doesn't want you to stay there.

So take away the "worry welcome mat." Let God calm your mind, comfort your heart, and care for your spirit. When you trust Him, worry has to leave. Oh sure, it will try to come back—but over time, you'll find you like God's comfort more than worry's distractions.

You have a choice to make: Will you let worry take over your thoughts, or will you turn to God in prayer? Will you think about those things that trouble you or think about God's Word?

Make the right choice. Turn your worries over to God, and He will make things better. His comfort will bring joy to your soul.

Lord, make me wise enough to stop worry before it calls my brain its home.

GREAT JOY

You have never seen [Jesus] but you love Him. You cannot see Him now but you are putting your trust in Him. And you have joy so great that words cannot tell about it.
1 Peter 1:8

How would you feel if you were forced to leave your own house and city and move to another country? That's what happened to the people Peter wrote to.

He sent a letter to Christians who had been persecuted and scattered to other countries. As hard as that must have been, Peter reminded the believers of their hope that never dies.

He wrote, "You are being kept by the power of God because you put your trust in Him and you will be saved from the punishment of sin at the end of the world. With this hope you can be happy even if you need to have sorrow and all kinds of tests for awhile" (1 Peter 1:5–6).

At times, all of us will have sorrow and tests. But if you've put your trust in Jesus, you'll never have to face punishment for your sin. That's a reason to feel great joy!

Lord Jesus, give me great joy, even in hard times.

PERFECT

You will keep the man in perfect peace whose mind is kept on You, because he trusts in You.

Isaiah 26:3

Imagine that God is a big, strong bodyguard, working all the time to keep you safe. The Bible says He will fill you with peace as you keep thinking about Him.

Beware of things that will take your mind off God. Sure, movies and video games and sporting events are fun. But if you spend all your time thinking about them, how will you keep your mind on God? Don't let yourself be distracted by the things of the world. If you want to have peace—if you want to be happy and content no matter what's going on around you—you'll have to keep your mind on God.

Look for His wonderful power in your life as He answers your prayers and provides everything you need. God cares deeply for you, and He wants what's best for your life. Remember to always make Him number one, and everything else will fall into place.

God, please help me trust You in everything. Help me remember that You know better than I do! Thank You for caring about me.

WHO IS LISTENING?

Always be ready to tell everyone who asks you why you believe as you do. Be gentle as you speak and show respect.
1 Peter 3:15

The apostle Paul traveled thousands of miles to share the good news of Jesus Christ. Toward the end of his life, he was under arrest and waiting to be killed.

But instead of being angry about that, he wrote these words to the church at Philippi: "Christian brothers, I want you to know that what has happened to me has helped spread the Good News. Everyone around here knows why I am in prison. It is because I preached about Jesus Christ. All the soldiers who work for the leader of the country know why I am here" (Philippians 1:12–13).

Paul could have grumbled or whined or talked angrily to the soldiers who guarded him. Instead, he was respectful and gentle. He told them about Jesus. And some of the guards—even some members of Caesar's household—accepted Jesus as their Lord!

Who is listening? It could be anyone. Always speak with respect.

Father, please help me to share my faith in a way that is humble and gentle.

WAITING FOR THE REWARD

"When you give, do not let your left hand know what your right hand gives. Your giving should be in secret. Then your Father Who sees in secret will reward you."
MATTHEW 6:3–4

It feels good to do nice things for others. People appreciate your help and think good things about you. They might say that you're a nice guy and tell others what a good person you are. There's nothing wrong with any of that. But none of those things are the best reward for doing good.

Jesus says that when you give to others, you should do it in secret. Don't let anyone know that the good deed was yours. Why? Well, if someone on earth praises you for being kind, you've already gotten your reward. There's nothing more. But if *God* is the only one who saw the good thing you did, then He'll give you a reward in heaven later.

It isn't easy to wait for rewards. But the rewards that God promises are always worth the wait.

Lord, help me to do good things for the right reasons. Remind me today that Your rewards are better than earthly praise.

DAY 183

GOD'S MARVELOUS, AMAZING KINDNESS

You must be kind to each other. Think of the other person. Forgive other people just as God forgave you because of Christ's death on the cross.
EPHESIANS 4:32

One day during recess, David's best friend accidentally kicked him. Without thinking, David hit him in the face. Both of them were sent to the principal's office.

David was embarrassed. At first he felt like blaming Steve. But then he remembered what he was learning about God's marvelous, amazing kindness.

When he was asked what happened, David spoke up truthfully. "It wasn't Steve's fault. He accidentally kicked me. It was my fault for hitting him in the face. I'm really sorry."

Things were already bad enough, and David didn't want his best friend to get in trouble too. In the end, the principal let them both go back to class with just a warning. What a relief!

When you think about God's amazing kindness, it helps you do the right thing—even on your hardest day.

Lord, I want to think a lot more often about Your marvelous kindness. Remind me of what You did for me through Jesus' death on the cross.

DECIDE THEN FOLLOW

He [Moses] chose to suffer with God's people instead of having fun doing sinful things for awhile.
Hebrews 11:25

There are fun, cool, and popular people we want to be friends with. But sometimes they don't make good choices. If you do what they do, your choices won't be the choices God wants you to make.

In the Bible, Moses was adopted into the home of Egypt's king. But first he'd been born into God's family. When Moses grew up, he chose not to be known as a prince of Egypt but as someone who followed God.

You might be known as a boy who's good at baseball or lives in a nice house. You could be known as a boy who doesn't play sports at all or never talks about where he lives. None of that is as important as following God.

Sinful things—bad choices—can be fun. For a while. But the Bible says the end of them is death (Proverbs 14:12). Follow Moses' example: Decide how you're going to live. Then follow the Lord.

Father, help me choose You instead of the people who do not follow You. I don't want to get lost.

DAY 185

KNOCK DOWN YOUR TOWER

Then they said, "Come, let us build a city for ourselves, with a tower that touches the heavens. Let us make a name for ourselves, or else we may be sent everywhere over the whole earth."

GENESIS 11:4

After the great flood, God blessed Noah and commanded his sons and their wives to "have many children, and cover the earth" (Genesis 9:1). Many generations later, people rebelled. They didn't want to "cover the earth," so they decided to build a tower right where they lived. (Maybe they thought that would keep them safe from another flood.) The Lord's response was to mix up the people's language and scatter them all over the whole earth—just like He originally planned.

It's never a good idea to go against God's commands. But when we trust our own limited understanding, we often do the opposite of what God says. We think it's safer to do our own thing, so we build ourselves a tower. That didn't work for the people in Genesis 11, and it won't work for us either. Brave boys knock down those towers. Do what God says!

Lord, may I always do what You say right away.

TINY TO GOD

What the Lord had told His servant Moses to do, he told Joshua, and Joshua did it. He did everything the Lord had told Moses.

JOSHUA 11:15

Many, many years ago there was a brave young man named Joshua. God used him to do great things.

Why? Because Joshua knew how to obey God.

The Lord told Joshua to find new land for the Israelites. Many people were afraid, but Joshua had faith. He led the Israelites to a city named Jericho, which they marched around seven times. Then they blew trumpets and shouted—and watched the giant walls fall, just like God had said they would. Joshua and the people quickly took over the land.

Are there any giant walls in your life? Maybe it's a class at school or some job you don't feel confident doing. Maybe it's a person who doesn't treat you well. Just do what God says and see how He takes care of your problem. What's big to you is tiny to God.

Lord, I want to be brave like Joshua. Sometimes I feel nervous that I'm not strong enough. Thank You for reminding me that my problems are tiny to You.

NOT WHAT YOU EXPECTED?

Naaman was very angry and went away. He said, "I thought he would come out to me, and stand, and call on the name of the Lord his God. I thought he would wave his hand over the place, and heal the bad skin disease."

2 Kings 5:11

We humans have a bad habit of wanting to tell God what to do and how to do it. That's kind of like an ant marching up to you and making demands. Crazy, huh?

In the Old Testament, Naaman made that mistake. He had a skin disease called leprosy, and someone told him that the prophet Elisha could help. Naaman was from the country of Syria. Elisha sent a messenger to tell him to wash in Israel's Jordan River to be healed.

Naaman, a powerful army commander, couldn't believe it. *Why didn't Elisha himself come out? Why can't I wash in the rivers of Syria instead?*

Happily for Naaman, one of his servants convinced him to do what Elisha said. And Naaman was completely healed.

When God's ways don't make sense, trust Him anyway. He always knows best.

Lord, may I always do what You say, even when I don't understand.

DAY 188

BOW NOW OR BOW LATER

The Holy Writings say, "As I live, says the Lord, every knee will bow before Me. And every tongue will say that I am God."
ROMANS 14:11

God is very kind. He's very generous. He's very patient. He's eager for everyone—including you!—to come to Him for salvation through His Son, Jesus Christ.

But God is also holy. That means He hates sin. Even though He allows bad things to happen for now, a day is coming when God's patience will be over. In that day, He will make everyone bow before Him. He will force everyone to admit that He, and He alone, is God.

That will be a scary time for people who have ignored or resisted God. But it will be a wonderful time for those of us who love and follow Jesus. After all the years of serving Him by faith—believing in Jesus even though we can't see Him—on that day we'll see Him, hear His voice, and feel His love in a bigger and better way than ever.

We will all bow before Jesus. Why not bow now?

Lord Jesus, I bow before You now in thanks and worship.

CAN'T BE BOUGHT

The man said to Joab, "Even for a thousand pieces of silver in my hand, I would not go against the king's son."
2 Samuel 18:12

Would any amount of money tempt you to do something wrong?

In 2 Samuel 18, King David's son Absalom was trying to steal the kingdom from his father. David's soldiers and Absalom's men were fighting a civil war. But David still loved his son and told his soldiers to spare Absalom's life.

One of David's captains, Joab, thought Absalom should die. And when he found a man who knew where Absalom was, he asked, "Why did you not kill him. . . . I would have given you ten pieces of silver" (verse 11). The honorable man responded with the words of today's verse. He wouldn't have killed the king's son for a *thousand* pieces of silver!

It seems like many people would do anything for money. That's not the way God's children should be. Right is right, wrong is wrong, and God will take care of us, no matter what. If money ever tempts you, just say, "Nope—I can't be bought!"

Father, remind me that You will meet all my needs.

DAY 190

WHERE DID THE BIBLE COME FROM?

"Take a book and write in it all the words which I have said to you about Israel, Judah, and all the nations. Write all I have said since the day I first spoke to you."
JEREMIAH 36:2

Whole books have been written to explain how we got the Bible. But this verse from Jeremiah gives a quick, clear answer to the question above.

Before he was even born, Jeremiah was chosen to be a prophet. Prophets got messages from God and then shared them with other people. God told Jeremiah to write down everything he'd been told to say. Jeremiah obeyed. Since then his writings have been copied, shared, and translated into many languages so that we can know just what God told him some 2,700 years ago.

When you read the Bible, you can be sure it's the Word of God. You can be sure that it's important, true, and powerful. You can be sure it will change your life if you let it.

Do you want to be a brave boy? Dig into God's Word every day.

Thank You, Lord, for giving us Your Word. I know I can trust it!

A BIGGER FAMILY

"Whoever does what My father in heaven wants him to do is My brother and My sister and My mother."
MATTHEW 12:50

If you follow Jesus, your family is much bigger than your parents, brothers, or sisters—or even your grandparents, cousins, aunts, and uncles. Everyone who sees life the way God does and accepts His great rescue plan through Jesus is a brother or sister. God's family is *huge*, and it gets bigger every time someone is saved.

If you ever feel alone, remember that you have family in every country in the world. While you're not born into God's family (you have to be *born again*), you can choose to become family—and family members should work together.

Jesus said that when men and women, boys and girls do what His Father wants them to do, He considers them to be His family. He wants you to belong! And He wants you to know that you are never truly alone.

Lord, please give me courage to reach out to others who love You. When I am shy, make me bold. When I am busy, remind me that my Christian family is important.

DAY 192

TWO CAN STAND

One man is able to have power over him who is alone, but two can stand against him. It is not easy to break a rope made of three strings.
Ecclesiastes 4:12

Some people in Australia made an interesting video. They interviewed several students, asking how they would describe themselves. The students spoke badly of themselves, repeating things they'd probably heard from bullies over the years. But then they got to see and hear a video of things their classmates had said about them. They heard compliments, kind words that made them feel good inside and even changed their lives. The video ends with this message: "Your words are powerful. Use them for good."

When the Bible says that two can stand against one, this is what it's talking about. If you stand up for a friend—if you stand with him against someone who is mistreating him—you can change his life. Be quick to tell everyone, but especially those who have been bullied, about the positive things you see in them. It'll make a real difference.

Father, please give me courage always to stand up for those who are mistreated.

DAY 193

SET YOUR HOPE

Set your hope now and forever on the loving-favor to be given you when Jesus Christ comes again.
1 PETER 1:13

For many kids, childhood is a time of learning, playing, goofing around—and not too much stress. But as you get older, you'll realize that life is *not* all fun and games. Really, it can be downright hard. Want proof? Ask your parents or grandparents if they ever struggled to pay bills, worried over a health problem, or wished their kids behaved better. (Yeah, buddy, we're looking at you!)

Part of growing up is dealing with hard things. For most kids, moms or dads or grandparents or teachers protect them from the worst stresses. But the day will come when you're on your own.

Well, not totally on your own. If you're a Christian, you always have Jesus with you. And the Bible says you can "set your hope" on the loving-favor He'll bring when He returns to earth. Whatever hard things you face—now as a kid or later as an adult—will be completely forgotten in Jesus' happy forever.

Lord, thank You for the hope of eternity. It makes me brave in this life!

DAY 194

BETTER BREAD

Jesus said to them, "This is the work of God, that you put your trust in the One He has sent."
JOHN 6:29

After He fed thousands of people with five loaves of barley bread and a couple small fish, Jesus was pretty popular. So after He went across the lake, some of those five thousand people who ate the miraculous lunch followed Him and asked Him for more. They didn't necessarily want to follow Jesus—they just wanted more food.

Jesus loves to take care of people's needs. But He knows the thing people need most is to trust in Him. Now, trusting God isn't always easy—it requires dedication. You'll have to work at it. But when you put your trust in God, He'll give you a lot more than free bread. He'll give you the bread of eternal life, which feeds your soul instead of your belly.

When you stop to thank God for the food you eat, thank Him for something else—the spiritual food of His Word and Holy Spirit.

Thank You, Lord, for taking care of my physical needs. Thank You even more for filling me up with Your love.

DAY 195

GOD IS SPEAKING. ARE YOU LISTENING?

Then I heard the voice of the Lord, saying, "Whom should I send? Who will go for Us?" Then I said, "Here am I. Send me!"
Isaiah 6:8

One Sunday David's pastor stopped in the middle of his sermon. Curious, David looked up. Imagine his huge surprise when the pastor spoke again, saying, "I want to talk about young David. I believe God will use him in big ways. I believe David will help thousands of people to know what God says in the Bible." David shook his head. No, he wasn't dreaming. The pastor really said that!

Now imagine if *your* pastor stopped his sermon and said something like that about you. How would you feel? You'd probably feel a lot of things! And how long would you remember what he said? Probably for the rest of your life.

As you read Bible verses, don't be surprised if you sense God saying, "Hey, this verse is for you. This is one way I want to use you to help thousands of people." Yes, *you*!

Lord, I welcome You to speak to me. When You do, I promise to listen!

DO YOU NEED REMINDERS?

When Abram was ninety-nine years old, the Lord came to him and said, "I am God All-powerful. Obey Me, and be without blame."
Genesis 17:1

At home, does your mom or dad ever have to remind you of what you should do? Of course. At practice, does the coach or band director ever need to remind you how to improve your playing? That's why we have coaches and band directors. At school, does your teacher ever have to remind you about your assignments? For most people, yep.

Have you ever wondered, *How soon until I don't need reminders all the time?* Well, if Abram (later known as Abraham) is any example, it appears people need reminders as long as they live. He was *ninety-nine* when God said, "Obey Me"!

Like Abraham, we all need reminders of what to do, what is true, and who the Lord is. It's not enough to know these things "once upon a time." We need to keep remembering God's truth each and every day. (That's why it's great that you're reading this book.)

Lord, today I'm glad to be reminded that You are God. Don't let me forget how to please You!

FREEZE, FEAR!

"Do not be afraid. For those who are with us are more than those who are with them."
2 Kings 6:16

When your grandfather was your age, the games he played were probably different than the games you play. One game from way back when is called "Capture the Flag." It's an outdoor contest, kind of like freeze tag, in which players try to snatch the flag of the other team without being captured themselves. If you had an extra-large team and could say the words of today's verse—"Those who are with us are more than those who are with them"—you'd be in good shape to win.

Knowing you have help can make you courageous. The prophet Elisha spoke the words above, and he said them because he knew God was with him. God sent help when things were hard. With God's help, Elisha won.

You might feel alone, but God *never* leaves you on your own. And He helps in ways you never thought possible. Because of this, you can freeze fear in its tracks.

Lord God, I can't always see the help You send, but when You do, I love the results.

THE POOR HELPING THE POOR

They have been put to the test by much trouble, but they have much joy. They have given much even though they were very poor.
2 CORINTHIANS 8:2

In the apostle Paul's time, there were churches in several cities of Macedonia—cities like Philippi, Thessalonica, and Berea. Those churches had gone through some tough times. John Wesley, a famous preacher in the 1700s, believed that the Macedonian churches had been "continually persecuted, harassed, and plundered"—that means they had everything *stolen* from them! Even so, their joy in the Lord led them to give much to help other poor people.

When you go through tough times, are you still joyful? Can you remember how God has met your needs in the past? Would you be as willing as the Macedonian churches to help others, even when you feel poor?

That would be a brave thing to do. And if you can, expect people who don't know Jesus to take notice. Who knows? They might even choose to follow Jesus too!

Lord, I want to be like the Christians in Macedonia—people who gave even when they didn't have much.

LIKE A ROCK

My heart will not be moved, O God. My heart cannot be moved. I will sing, yes, I will sing praises!
Psalm 57:7

Have you heard of the Rock of Gibraltar? It's a gigantic mass of stone in the Mediterranean Sea, just off the southern coast of Spain. About three miles long and not quite a mile wide, it rises almost 1,400 feet at its highest point. When people want to describe something that's solid and unmoving, they say it's like "the Rock."

And that's how David, the psalm writer, described his love for God. Some people wanted to hurt David—in fact, the king, Saul, was trying to *kill* him. But David knew God had already protected him and would continue to keep him safe. Because of that, David said his heart could not be moved away from his God. He was as firm as the Rock of Gibraltar!

You can be too. If you follow Jesus, God is your Father. He will provide for your needs on earth, then take you home to heaven where everything is perfect. So be strong, like a rock.

Father God, may my heart never be moved from You.

BE ON WATCH

"Be sure you watch. Pray all the time so that you may be able to keep from going through all these things that will happen and be able to stand before the Son of Man."
LUKE 21:36

In ancient times, there was a very important job in cities and villages. The watchman stood at a gate or on top of a wall and kept an eye out for threats to the community. That might sound like an easy job, but it took some very strong eyes at nighttime, when all the watchman had was firelight.

God has called us to watch too. We keep an eye out for threats to ourselves and the people we care about. And we pray. We don't have control over the bad things in life, but through prayer, we can talk to the one who *is* in control! We can ask God to watch over our families and friends, our teachers, neighbors, and classmates.

Be sure you watch. Pray all the time. Ask God to protect you and your loved ones.

Lord God, help me to be alert to the dangers of this world. Protect me and my family and friends, I pray.

DON'T MAKE BIG PROMISES

"You have heard that it was said long ago,
'You must not make a promise you cannot keep.
You must carry out your promises to the Lord.'"
MATTHEW 5:33

Imagine promising your dad or mom that you'll clean your room perfectly every day. Is that a wise promise to make? No. Why not? Because "perfectly" and "every day" are just too much. It would be much better simply to clean your room before your parents tell you to. That way you'll pleasantly surprise them. They'll be much happier than if you promised a "perfectly" clean room "every day."

It's the same way with God. Really, just do the right thing. Do what God wants you to do, as He's told you in the Bible. Then relax. You don't have to tell God what you did. And you certainly don't want to promise Him that you'll do right "perfectly" and "every day." That's just too much this side of heaven.

Lord, I see why I shouldn't make big (or even medium-sized) promises to You. I'll simply do what You want. I could never surprise You anyway!

DAY 202

DOING GOOD, QUIETLY

If someone has the gift of speaking words of comfort and help, he should speak. If someone has the gift of sharing what he has, he should give from a willing heart.
ROMANS 12:8

Words like *brave*, *bold*, and *courageous* seem to describe guys fighting a battle or running toward a burning skyscraper. But the terms apply to other people too.

There is godly courage in doing good quietly. In Romans 12, the apostle Paul wrote about some spiritual gifts that hardly anyone sees. God might have given you the gift of "speaking words of comfort and help," and that's usually a one-on-one thing. A lonely kid on the playground needs you, and you step up to be a friend.

Or maybe God gave you the gift of sharing what you have. You follow Jesus' command to do it secretly—you don't "blow a horn" as He said in Matthew 6:2. But whatever you give quietly, God can use in big, bold ways.

Kind, generous, quiet boys are also brave. And God always notices.

Father, I'm thankful that I don't have to fight lions or giants to be brave. Help me to courageously and quietly help others.

DREAMS GONE BAD

[Jesus] said to them, "What would you like to have Me do for you?" They said to Him, "Let one of us sit by Your right side and the other by Your left side when You receive Your great honor in heaven."
MARK 10:36–37

Even great people make mistakes. Jesus' closest friend, John, once asked for something really dumb: He and his brother James wanted the two most important seats in heaven.

James and John were among the first people Jesus chose as disciples. They traveled with Him, learned from Him, and served Him and others in many ways. The brothers were part of the "advance team" that started Christianity—all the millions (possibly *billions*) of people over the centuries who have followed Jesus. That's a worthwhile dream.

But James and John lost focus. They started thinking of themselves more than Jesus. Their dream went bad, and Jesus had to remind them of the real issue—Himself.

The best dreams are those that honor Jesus by pointing people to Him. When that's your goal, everyone wins. Just be sure to keep sight of the goal!

**Lord, give me good dreams—
and keep me focused on You.**

THAT KIND OF LAW

Help each other in troubles and problems.
This is the kind of law Christ asks us to obey.
GALATIANS 6:2

When you choose to love other people, you're making a very brave decision. They might show love in return, but some could make fun of you. Those people might even say they don't *need* any friends, but don't believe them. Everyone needs friends.

They might just be going through a very hard time. Sometimes people think it's easier to push away people who want to help than admit they actually need help. But you can win them over with love. Love listens, sticks around on hard days, and cheers like crazy when good things happen.

This love is real. It's trustworthy. It protects. It sticks around long after the first awkward moment, when the other guy tries to ignore you.

Love helps—and that's just the kind of law God wants you to obey.

Lord, You asked me to love. That's not complicated, but it's hard. It's easier to think about my own needs and the things I want to do. Please help me to be brave enough to do the hard thing.

SANCTI-WHAT?

May the God of peace set you apart for Himself. May every part of you be set apart for God. May your spirit and your soul and your body be kept complete. May you be without blame when our Lord Jesus Christ comes again.
1 Thessalonians 5:23

Ever hear the word *sesquipedalian*? It's a long word that describes long words. And it's extra funny when you understand what it says in the original language of Latin. "Sesquipedalian" literally means "foot and a half long."

Now here's a foot-and-a-half-long Bible word for you: *sanctification*. It means "to be set apart for God." (In fact, that's exactly how the Bible used in this devotional—the New Life Version—handles the word.) When you become a Christian, God "sets you apart" from the world. You have different goals, different desires, and a different future. You make different choices to keep your mind and soul and body safe and healthy. You keep moving farther from the world and closer to God.

At least that's the way brave boys live their lives.

Father God, I want You to sanctify me—to set me apart for Yourself—in this world.

NEW-DAY JOY

Crying may last for a night, but joy comes with the new day.
Psalm 30:5

Imagine you're going to bed when a loud, flashing thunderstorm blows in. The windows rattle from the wind, the lightning bolts are close enough to sizzle, and the thunder rumbles so heavily you can feel it in your chest. The storm just goes on and on until, somehow, you fall asleep.

But when you wake up, everything is calm. The sun is shining, the birds are singing, the storm is history. In fact, the world feels like a fresh new place. The rain has washed the dirt off the sidewalks, the grass and flowers are brighter, even the people in your neighborhood seem to be happier.

That's a good picture of the Christian life. This world can be a sad, hard place. There are all kinds of "storms," and whether we want to admit it or not, we feel like crying. But God promises good to His children. He'll bring joy with the new day—whether that's actually tomorrow or the "new day" of eternity. If you're a Christian, you really can't lose!

God, please give me a happy heart in this sad world.

BOAZ AND RUTH

"Pull some grain out of the grain that has been gathered together and leave it for her to gather. And do not speak sharp words to her."

RUTH 2:16

Boaz was a nice guy who lived in some not-so-nice times. His story happened before Israel had a king, so no one was really enforcing God's laws. Still, Boaz was a good man who cared about justice and kindness.

Ruth was a nice girl from Moab. She was taking care of her mother-in-law, Naomi, even though she didn't have to. Ruth's and Naomi's husbands had both died, and they were poor widows who had to depend on the kindness of others for food to eat. Ruth went through farm fields that had already been harvested to pick up whatever grain had been left behind.

When Boaz saw the kindness Ruth showed to Naomi, he showed kindness to her. He told his field workers to leave out some extra grain for Ruth.

Kindness is always a choice, but it's an easier choice when others are kind too. Why not start a chain of kindness with the people you see today?

Lord, help me to be like Boaz and Ruth.

LOOK FOR GOOD MEN TO FOLLOW

Christian brothers, live your lives as I have lived mine. Watch those who live as I have taught you to live.
PHILIPPIANS 3:17

Experience is the best teacher—especially the experiences of other people. What that means is that life is too short to learn everything the hard way. Instead, watch what others do and learn from *their* mistakes and successes. That will save you a lot of unnecessary pain and suffering, which is good. It will also help you to know how to do what is good and right, whatever is best in God's eyes. That's even better!

Do you know someone who loves the Lord wholeheartedly? Who around you loves other people well? Who do you see as wise and kind? Maybe it's one of your parents or grandparents. Maybe it's a coach or a teacher. Maybe it's a Sunday school or youth group leader. Whoever it is, learn all you can from that person—things to help you live happily for God all your days.

Lord, I thank You for putting good, godly men in my life. Please help me to learn a lot from them.

REMEMBER WHO YOU ARE

Jonah said to them, "I am a Hebrew, and I worship the Lord God of heaven Who made the sea and the dry land."
JONAH 1:9

If you grew up in church, probably one of the first stories you heard was "Jonah and the whale." We can learn a lot from Jonah's example—things like *Don't disobey God!* But today's verse shows us something good about the man: He knew who (and whose) he was.

Though Jonah was running away from God, he answered truthfully when asked who he was. Jonah knew that he came from the one true God, the Creator of the dry land and the wild, stormy ocean that was threatening to sink the ship he was on. "I worship the Lord God of heaven," he said.

And so do we. Never forget that, as a Christian, you worship the one true God. In fact, it's even better than that—*you're His child!* As the apostle Paul wrote, "God already planned to have us as his own children. This was done by Jesus Christ" (Ephesians 1:5).

Father, thank You for making me Your own. May I never forget who I am in Christ!

GOD GOES WITH YOU

For I know that nothing can keep us from the love of God. Death cannot! Life cannot! Angels cannot! Leaders cannot! Any other power cannot! Hard things now or in the future cannot! The world above or the world below cannot! Any other living thing cannot keep us away from the love of God which is ours through Christ Jesus our Lord.

Romans 8:38–39

Think about all the things you worry about. Got them in mind? Good. Now, which ones are beyond God's power? Spiders? Nope, God can handle anything with eight legs. Darkness? Ha! God can see in the dark. Your family has to move to another town? It's okay—God's going with you.

Nothing you can imagine would ever take you away from God's love. *Nothing*. You can't even run away from God, because He's already there wherever you go.

Whatever makes you afraid is so much smaller than God's love. That love means you don't have to worry about anything. When you're tempted to worry, read today's verse over and over again.

God, when I feel like I'm all alone, please help me to look for You. Your love never leaves me.

COUNT YOUR BLESSINGS

Happy are the people who have all this.
Yes, happy are the people whose God is the Lord!
Psalm 144:15

One of the wonderful things about the book of Psalms is that it's so real. We read about people who had problems just like we do. But they still found ways to worship God and find their happiness in Him.

In Psalm 144, the writer made a long list of good things in his life. He reminded himself of God's loving-kindness, His strength, His protection, and His saving power. Then the psalm writer asked for blessing over his children, his storehouses of food, and his livestock. Happy are the people who have all this, he said. Happy are the people whose God is the Lord!

Get a sheet of paper and make your own list of reasons to be happy. It's okay if it looks different than the psalm writer's. Your list might include your parents, your friends, a safe place to sleep at night, your favorite foods. . . Keep going—you'll be amazed at what God does for you.

Lord, when I count my blessings,
I'm happy that You've taken
such good care of me.

YOUR SAFE PLACE

"Good will come to the man who trusts in the Lord, and whose hope is in the Lord."
JEREMIAH 17:7

God wants you always to trust Him. Your enemy, the devil, wants to tempt you into believing the *world* will meet your needs. Don't believe that—it's simply not true.

God is your safe place. He is the one who gave you life and who offers you eternal life through Jesus. He is the one who provides food, clothing, and shelter—He created those things and hands them down to you through parents and other concerned adults. He is the one who invented love and joy and all good things and invites you to find hope in Himself. Your trust in Him opens the door to blessing.

When you're tempted to worry whether you have enough, or to envy the things other people have, or even to lie and cheat to get more, remind yourself of Jeremiah 17:7. Trust in the Lord, and good will come. He is your safe place.

Lord Jesus, teach me how to trust You when things get tough. Help me to face hard times knowing that You always provide.

UNDERSTAND THEN FORGIVE

Try to understand other people. Forgive each other. If you have something against someone, forgive him. That is the way the Lord forgave you.
Colossians 3:13

Kelson was excited. His dad had scheduled a business trip, and he invited Kelson to come along. And not just any business trip—it was five days in *Hawaii*. On the second day, Kelson and his dad drove to a jungle about half an hour from the hotel. At his dad's encouragement, Kelson started swinging on a vine. It was great fun as he flew faster and higher.

Great fun, that is, until the vine snapped. Kelson landed flat on his back. He couldn't breathe! His dad picked him up, and the air finally rushed back into Kelson's lungs.

Kelson's dad hugged him and encouraged him to grab another vine. Kelson thought, *No way!* until his dad said, "This time, however, *I'm* going to test the vine to make sure it won't break."

Dad never intended to hurt his son. When Kelson realized that, he was happy to grab the next vine his dad tested. Understand then forgive!

Lord, sometimes Mom or Dad makes a mistake. Help me to understand then forgive.

NO PAYBACKS

"Whoever hits you on one side of the face, turn so he can hit the other side also. Whoever takes your coat, give him your shirt also."
LUKE 6:29

Whew, here's a hard verse from the Bible!

Jesus commanded some tough things in His Sermon on the Mount. How on earth are we supposed to do what He says in Luke 6:29? Two quick thoughts:

First, we *can't* do what Jesus says if we're trying to do these things in our own strength. It has to be God who gives us the restraint to keep from fighting back.

Second, some people think the idea of "fighting back"—that is, planning revenge—is really what Jesus was talking about here. Jesus didn't mean that we should just let bad people do anything they want to us, but that when someone mistreats us, we don't try to find ways to get them back. Revenge is a poison that hurts everyone.

It takes a brave boy to stop the cycle of insults and violence. But if you ask, God will gladly help you.

Father, please help me to be like Jesus—willing to forgive the bad things other people do to me.

LAW KEEPERS

"I tell you, as long as heaven and earth last, not one small mark or part of a word will pass away of the Law of Moses until it has all been done."
MATTHEW 5:18

In some ways, it's simple to be a Christian. You just have to believe that Jesus died on the cross to pay for the sins you committed. Here's how the apostle Paul explained it: "If you say with your mouth that Jesus is Lord, and believe in your heart that God raised Him from the dead, you will be saved from the punishment of sin" (Romans 10:9).

"Getting saved" is all about what we *believe*, not what we *do*. But here's where some people get confused. Though we don't have to obey rules to become saved, once we have become Christians, God wants us to follow His rules. That's what Jesus meant in Matthew 5:18. Long-ago rules against stealing, lying, and even coveting (wanting something that someone else has) are still in effect.

Brave boys know and keep God's law.

Lord, please help me to understand Your law. Keeping it doesn't save me, but when I'm saved I should keep it.

STEP FORWARD TOGETHER

So Moses stood in the gate of the place where they had set up their tents and said, "Whoever is for the Lord, come to me!" And all the sons of Levi came together around him.
EXODUS 32:26

You don't choose to follow God based on how popular He is with all the kids in school. What if most kids *don't* follow God?

One time, God's people were really messing up. Their leader, Moses, wanted those who really followed God to join him outside their tents. Several men stepped forward and did a really hard job to fix the problem. God blessed them for their courage.

When you choose to follow God, you may think you're all alone. But most of the time, that's not true. Be courageous and follow even when you think you're all God has. Then don't be surprised when others step forward to serve with you.

Lord God, it's lonely to think I am the only one following You. But I know You have many people who still want to do right. Thanks for helping me to see that I have friends.

KILL YOUR PRIDE

Peter spoke with strong words, "Even if I have to die with You, I will never say that I do not know You." All the followers said the same thing.
MARK 14:31

Peter was one of Jesus' closest friends. He was also what people call a "loose cannon"—someone who acts and speaks without really thinking.

That's probably the best way to describe what happened in Mark 14. Jesus had just finished His "Last Supper" with the disciples on the night before He would die for the sins of the world. After dinner they all went out to the Mount of Olives, where Jesus said each of the disciples would leave Him!

Peter spoke up quickly. "I will never say that I do not know You," he insisted, promising even to *die* with Jesus. But you know the story: Just as Jesus predicted, Peter denied the Lord three times that night.

Be careful what you say—especially when you feel strongly about something. You might end up making a promise you cannot keep. It's better to stay silent and kill your pride than to speak up boastfully and commit a sin.

Lord, please keep me from prideful words.

LEARN TO OBEY

Even being God's Son, [Jesus] learned to obey by the things He suffered.
HEBREWS 5:8

Jesus is the perfect example of what an obedient, brave life looks like. He left His throne in heaven to come to earth and save people from their sins. He was born in a stable and grew to boyhood obeying His parents, Mary and Joseph. Then, as a grown-up, Jesus obeyed His heavenly Father, healing people from their physical and spiritual sickness. He constantly showed people what it looked like to trust God.

Jesus obeyed His Father by showing love to unpopular people. He helped those who couldn't help themselves. He fed people who were hungry, and He taught people who wanted to learn to please God. Even when the time came for Jesus to die on a cross, He obeyed—and He took the whole world's sin on His shoulders.

We can learn a lot from Jesus. And one great thing is that *we can learn to obey*. If you have trouble obeying and doing the brave thing, take heart. Jesus learned, and so can you!

Father God, thank You for Jesus. I want to learn to obey like He did.

FREEDOM TO [OR FROM] SIN

Christian brother, you were chosen to be free. Be careful that you do not please your old selves by sinning because you are free. Live this free life by loving and helping others.
GALATIANS 5:13

When Jesus died on the cross, He took the punishment for every sin you have ever done—and for every sin you ever will do. You are now free to choose how you'd like to live.

On one hand, you could do all kinds of bad things. Hey, Jesus has already been punished for them! But you already know that's not the right way to go.

On the other hand, you could be thankful for the fact that someone else took your punishment, and you can look for ways to pay that kindness forward. Or, as today's verse says, "by loving and helping others."

When you are free to do what you want, remember who died to give you that freedom. Then live for Him!

Lord Jesus, I thank You for dying for me. Help me to live for You. Give me the same love for others that You have shown to me.

HONORABLE MEN

How happy are the sons of a man who is right with God and walks in honor!
Proverbs 20:7

If you have a great dad, thank God. If your dad isn't so great—or not even around—trust God.

When men become fathers, they're supposed to "bring up a child by teaching him the way he should go" (Proverbs 22:6). Some men do a great job at that. Others don't.

We can't say exactly why God puts some boys in good homes and others in not-so-good homes. But we can say this for sure: God knows everything, and He doesn't make mistakes. So whether you're the happy son of "a man who is right with God" or you can only dream of such a thing, you're right where God put you. The big question is this: Will *you* become a man who "walks in honor"?

You can't change anyone but yourself. If your dad is great, follow his example. If your dad disappoints you, decide to become a better man. God, the perfect Father, will gladly help you to do that.

Lord, help me to become a man who is right with You, someone who walks in honor.

TODAY IS JESUS YOUR LORD?

"You call Me Teacher and Lord. You are right because that is what I am."
JOHN 13:13

Most people don't wake up in the morning and say, "I think I'm going to rebel against the Lord and mess up my life today." No, people often choose to sin by the small choices they make. How often do people read what the Bible says and then quietly decide, "I'm not so sure I believe that," or "I'm not quite ready to obey it."

When they do that, people deliberately ignore the hundreds of stories in the Bible. Those real-life stories show what happens when people either trust and obey the Lord or when they *dis*trust and *dis*obey Him. Good things happen when we trust and obey. When we don't? It gets ugly fast.

In the New Testament, the word *Lord* often refers to Jesus Christ, God's Son and our Savior. Calling Him "Lord" refers to the fact that He is supposed to be number one in our hearts and lives. If that's true for you, great! If not, it's time to pray.

Jesus, I want You to be Lord of my life today. Help me to trust and obey!

LOOKING FORWARD TO FOREVER

Bring up a child by teaching him the way he should go,
and when he is old he will not turn away from it.
PROVERBS 22:6

Parents spend time talking to babies so they learn what things are called and how they work. Over time, you were taught to sleep in your own bed, how to say letters and numbers, and what to do to get ready for school in the morning. Many moms and dads also work hard to help their kids know Jesus. Maybe a parent even gave you this book! Face it, they care about you.

God said that parents should teach their kids the right way to live. Later on, even as grown-ups, those kids will usually follow what they've learned—even after they've made some wrong decisions.

The hard work your parents are doing can help you look forward to forever, and it's always a good choice to say, "Thank you."

God, when my dad or mom wants to teach me good things about You, please help me to pay attention. May I take what I learn and make it a part of my life.

WHAT FRIENDS DO

"You are My friends if you do what I tell you."
John 15:14

Have you ever thought of Jesus as your friend? He's the Lord of the universe, able to command the seas and everything in them, yet He's also your *friend*.

How so? Well, friends always look out for each other. They put the other guy's needs and desires ahead of their own. They might even put their own lives on the line. In John 15:13, Jesus said, "No one can have greater love than to give his life for his friends." That's exactly what He did on the cross for you.

All true friendships have two-way love. If one person in a relationship makes all the sacrifices and does all the good deeds, he won't consider the other person a true friend. It's the same way with Jesus: As your friend, He gave up His life for you. Now He expects you to live for Him—to follow Him, obey Him, and love Him. That's what brave boys do.

Lord, I thank You for calling me a friend. Help me to show You how much I love You.

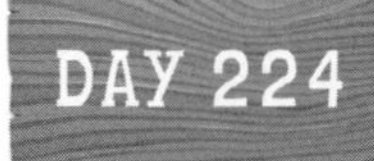

WHEN THE KING RETURNS

"I am coming very soon. Hold on to what you have so no one can take your crown."
REVELATION 3:11

In the last book of the Bible, Jesus talks to several churches in a place called Asia Minor. Some of those churches were not doing the right thing, and Jesus had to remind them to love God and love other people.

But one of the churches, in a city called Philadelphia, was doing well. Jesus complimented them for being patient and faithful. They obeyed His words, and Jesus promised to take care of them. Jesus also told the church at Philadelphia that He was going to return to earth one day. Until that time, they should always hold on to the truth.

That's something that we need to remember too, today and every day. Whatever is happening in our lives, whether it's good or bad, Jesus is coming. When the King returns, He'll make everything right. Hold on to His words and don't let go.

King Jesus, I thank You for taking care of Your church. Help me to hold on to Your words until that day You return to earth.

DAY 225

[NOT ALWAYS] HAPPY TO HELP

Those who plant with tears will gather fruit with songs of joy.
Psalm 126:5

Jonathan is busy constructing his latest Lego creation when Mom pops in to say, "Five minutes until dinner." Jonathan immediately heads to the bathroom to wash his hands and then asks his dad if he can set the table.

Um, no.

What really happens? Jonathan keeps playing. Mom eventually shouts, "One more minute!" Jonathan doesn't even look up. He knows his parents won't start eating without him. Besides, he wants to finish constructing one more part of his Mega Mars Mission Module before he breaks for dinner.

Can we let you in on a secret? Actually, *two* secrets: First, the Mega Mars Mission Module can wait. Second, surprising your mom or dad is actually great fun. Try it for yourself. Next time around, go to the dinner table *early*, offering to help. And don't ask for any reward—just enjoy your mom and dad's smiles.

Best of all? Imagine Jesus smiling too.

**Lord, I can be just like Jonathan.
Help me to learn the two secrets myself.**

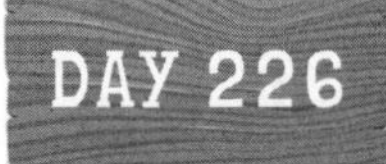

EYES TO THE BLIND

"I was eyes to the blind, and feet to the man who could not walk."
Job 29:15

The story of Job proves that bad things can happen to good people.

Job suffered losses that most people can only imagine—but don't want to. He lost his wealth, *and* his children, *and* his health in a very short time. He'd been targeted by Satan, and God allowed the devil to attack Job to prove that he would stay faithful.

Job didn't realize then that he was part of a much bigger story. He wondered why things were going so bad, when he'd always been so good. In today's verse, he recalled how he had taken care of blind and disabled people—and in verse 16 says he did that for strangers, not just friends.

We should be helpful too, no matter what's going on in our lives. When times are good, be helpful. When times are bad, be helpful. Someone else will appreciate it. You'll feel better. And God will notice and reward you—if not in this life, then in eternity.

Lord, I want to serve *You* by serving others. May I be eyes to the blind today.

DAY 227

THE THINGS GOD DOESN'T DO

"When you pass through the waters, I will be with you. When you pass through the rivers, they will not flow over you. When you walk through the fire, you will not be burned. The fire will not destroy you."
ISAIAH 43:2

You cannot go anywhere that takes you away from God. No matter where you are, He's there.

When you're in school and a bully is mean, God is there. When you're home and there's more schoolwork than you think you can handle, He's there. When you're in trouble with your mom or dad because of something you've done, He's there.

God doesn't show up only on days with blue skies. He's there on the days when you've messed up *again*. He's there when other people are rude. He's there to help you with your needs.

God will never leave you or act like you're a stranger or pretend He doesn't notice you. Other people might, but God doesn't do anything like that.

He's on your side. No fear required.

Lord, I want to have friends, and I'm disappointed when people let me down. Thanks for being my best friend. Thanks for noticing me.

DAY 228

TREAT ME RIGHT

A man who is right with God cares for his animal,
but the sinful man is hard and has no pity.
PROVERBS 12:10

Do you like pets? People in the United States sure do. According to the *World Atlas*, Americans keep more than 171 million freshwater fish, nearly 94 million cats, and almost 80 million dogs. There are also 15 million pet birds, nearly 14 million reptiles, and over 13 million horses.

Most people love their pets and treat them well. But not everyone—some people neglect and abuse animals. That's not what God intended.

The book of Proverbs says sinful people are harsh with animals. When you're right with God, you'll look out for creatures that are smaller and weaker than you. That would even include people!

Brave boys stand up for others and make sacrifices for them. If your dog needs to go out late at night, volunteer to do that. If you see a kid being bullied at school, step in to help. When you see a need, meet it—and God will be pleased.

Lord, I want to look out for those who need help. I want to treat everyone—animals and people—right.

BE GIVING AND FAIR

Good will come to the man who is ready to give much, and fair in what he does.
Psalm 112:5

What do you think? Would you like to know the kind of person this verse describes? Would you like to *be* that kind of person?

God's Word says that "good will come" to the person who is known for two things: First, he is "ready to give much." (Some Bible translations say this person deals generously and is willing to lend money to others.) Second, the person must be "fair in what he does."

Do you know anyone like this? Maybe your dad or your grandpa or an aunt or a teacher? Has good come to that person? Does God seem to be blessing him or her with money, food, and a good home? If so, imitate this person! Be like them in their generosity and their fair treatment of others.

Of course, nobody is perfect—but when you see someone courageous enough to live differently than the rest of the world, take note. This is how God wants *you* to live too.

Father God, please help me to be giving and fair.

A BRAND-NEW HEART

"I will give you a new heart and put a new spirit within you. I will take away your heart of stone and give you a heart of flesh."
EZEKIEL 36:26

The Bible says God gives His children a new heart. That doesn't mean the amazing little muscle in your chest that pumps blood around your body. (Did you know the heart beats two or three *billion* times in the average person's lifetime?) No, Ezekiel 36:26 means that God gives His children new desires. You will want to act like Jesus. You'll want to follow God's rules. You'll want to find ways to be a faithful Christian all the time.

Make studying your Bible a priority and decide to obey what God tells you. Look forward to quiet time with God every day, and you'll be amazed at how much He helps you and answers prayer.

When you're part of His family, God promises to bless you. He always watches over you to make sure you're okay. He'll make sure your new heart stays healthy.

Father in heaven, I thank You for the new heart that makes me true and brave.

FAITH PROTECTS

Most important of all, you need a covering of faith in front of you. This is to put out the fire-arrows of the devil.
Ephesians 6:16

In the Garden of Eden, the serpent fooled Adam and Eve by making them question God's word. "Did God say," the serpent asked, "that you should not eat from any tree in the garden?" (Genesis 3:1).

Eve answered that they could eat from any tree except the one called "the tree of the knowledge of good and evil." If they ate from that tree, she said, they would die. *Not true!* said the serpent. So Eve took fruit from the forbidden tree and ate it.

Adam and Eve should have shown more faith in the God who gave them the rules than in the serpent who made them question the rules. If they had, sin would have needed a different way to get into our world. Trusting God protects us from harm. When we listen to people who say something other than what God said, we put ourselves in danger.

Who are you going to listen to today?

Lord, keep me safe from the devil's attacks. Help me trust You more than anyone else.

ALWAYS THANKFUL

You must keep praying. Keep watching! Be thankful always.
Colossians 4:2

When you see the word *prayer*, what do you think of? Is it asking God for help in tough times? Is it asking for things we want? Prayer is both of those things, and more. Some of the most important prayers we can pray are those of thanksgiving. That just means we're saying "thank You" to God.

The book of Psalms is packed with prayers of thanksgiving. One is "For the Lord is good. His loving-kindness lasts forever. And He is faithful to all people and to all their children-to-come" (Psalm 100:5). If you have food on your dinner table, thank God. If you have strong legs for running and jumping, thank God. If you can see sunsets and sunrises, thank God. You can thank God on your skateboard or climbing a tree or when you're on vacation. You can be thankful in any and every situation!

God wants us to bring our requests to Him. But He's also happy to hear our "thank You" prayers too. In a selfish and ungrateful world, take a brave step—and always be thankful.

God, thank You!

MAKE A DIFFERENCE

Love each other as Christian brothers.
Show respect for each other.
ROMANS 12:10

Christians should be known for their choice to love each other. People should recognize you as a follower of Jesus because you care about others, treat people with respect, and help out when help is needed.

That's a pretty good picture of how Jesus wants you to follow Him. Those are all things that He does every day for you.

Have you ever wondered why love is such a big deal to God? Think about it: When you don't show love, you start wanting what other people have, you show disrespect, you wear a frown more often than a smile. Do you like hanging out with people like that? Most people don't.

God is working to make a difference in this world, so He asks *you* to be different too. It's a good difference, one that makes others want to know why you don't act like everyone else.

God, I want to do what others don't, because You've asked me to. I want to obey You by loving my Christian family. Maybe others will notice and want to know You too.

PAY UP!

When you make a promise to God, do not be late in paying it, for He is not pleased with fools. Pay what you promise to pay!
ECCLESIASTES 5:4

Grown-ups sometimes promise to give a lot of money to God if God will help them *make* a lot of money. It can sound like this: "God, if You make sure I land this million-dollar deal, I'll give twenty-five thousand dollars to the church." Or, "God, if You make sure I get a ten-thousand–dollar bonus by Christmas, I'll give two thousand to that new missionary."

What do you think? Is God tempted to answer these requests?

No, that's never what God does.

Here's what He wants: He wants men (and boys) to do the right thing. And He wants them to do the right thing in good times and bad. It's not right to think that making money is your biggest ambition. Instead, the right thing is giving some of your money *right now* to your church and missionaries.

When you give for God, He'll make sure that you're never in need.

**Lord, may I never be foolish.
Help me to give without hesitation.**

WALK IN OBEDIENCE

"See! I am coming soon. The one who obeys what is written in this Book is happy!"
Revelation 22:7

John 6:66–68 records a sad event. Many of Jesus' followers began to abandon Him, so He asked an important question of His twelve disciples: "Will you leave Me also?" Simon Peter's answer was the best one he could give: "Lord, who else can we go to? You have words that give life that lasts forever."

When you go to church, read your Bible, or even read books like this devotional, you're learning God's Word. But James 1:22 says you need to go one step further: "*Obey* the Word of God. If you hear only and do not act, you are only fooling yourself." As you obey, you'll turn your back on sin and find happiness as you walk closely with God.

The world will offer you things that give happiness for a short time. But so many of those things lead to sadness and heartache in the future. Only God can offer permanent happiness. Learn His Word—and then obey it.

Lord God, give me the power and grace I need to obey You.

SHINE BRIGHT

This is the reason we do not give up. Our human body is wearing out. But our spirits are getting stronger every day.
2 Corinthians 4:16

Never forget that God thinks you're special. You are a light for Him in a dark world where people have lost their way. Even though you'll have hard times yourself, don't let the struggles put out your flame.

Many people need to hear from you about Jesus. Other believers will look to you for encouragement. God will give you strength to serve both Christians and yet-to-be Christians. That's why the apostle Paul told us not to give up—he wanted as many people as possible to know God, and to give Him thanks.

When troubles come and you feel tired and weak, ask God to keep you shining bright. Keep praying, keep studying His Word, and God will make your spirit stronger every day.

Lord God, please give me the desire to read my Bible—and really study it. Help me to know You and be a light in my world. I want to lead people to Jesus.

A DAY TO SAY "THANK YOU!"

I remember your true faith. It is the same faith your grandmother Lois had and your mother Eunice had. I am sure you have that same faith also.
2 TIMOTHY 1:5

Bruce is a sports star who is super relaxed most of the time. But right before he performs his superhero-style stunts, Bruce is hyperfocused. How does he switch on and off so quickly? Bruce credits his mom. He says he developed his amazing ability to pay attention and react while he was studying classical piano with her. Oh, and Bruce's mom did something else that was very important: She shared her love of Jesus with her son.

Maybe your mom loves Jesus Christ with all her heart too. Or maybe it's your dad or one of your grandparents. Maybe it's all of the adults in your family. Whoever it is, today would be a great day to thank them. Just say, "Thank you for your faith in Jesus Christ. It means a lot to me." Then watch them smile!

Lord, it's easier to put my faith in You when someone else in my family did that first. I want to be thankful for each one.

I'M TIRED OF BEING KIND!

If someone has the gift of showing kindness to others, he should be happy as he does it.
ROMANS 12:8

Would anyone actually say they get tired of being kind?

Well, even if we don't say it, we sometimes *think* it. Why else would the apostle Paul write, "Do not let yourselves get tired of doing good" (Galatians 6:9)? It's why Paul wrote today's verse.

Every Christian should be kind. But God gives some followers of Jesus a special ability—a gift—to *really* show kindness. Many times, we feel good when we're kind to others. But there are also times when people don't respond like we think they should. They don't say "thanks." They don't seem to care. They might even be rude to us. Ugh!

It doesn't matter. God, through the apostle Paul, says, "Keep showing kindness. Be happy as you do." Those other people might finally appreciate us, or they might not. But God always will.

Tired of being kind? Ask God for help to keep at it—happily.

Lord, You know how difficult people can be. Please give me strength to be kind and to enjoy the fact that I'm really serving You.

HE CAN BE TRUSTED

Trust in the Lord with all your heart, and do not trust in your own understanding. Agree with Him in all your ways, and He will make your paths straight.
PROVERBS 3:5–6

Have you ever lied, taken something that didn't belong to you. or made fun of someone? Have you ever disobeyed, cheated, or wanted to punch another person? If you said yes to even one of those things (and we've *all* done some of them), it's pretty hard to trust yourself.

The only person we can always trust to make the right decisions is God. Because He knows everything, He *can* always make good choices. Because He loves His children completely, He *will* always make good choices. We can always trust God, even though we can't really trust ourselves.

Don't waste time trying to figure out life by yourself. Whether your choices are small (like whether to cheat on a board game) or big (like what you want to do with your life), God has a better answer. Trust Him to guide you.

Father, You can give me courage and help me reach my best goals. Help me to trust You in all my ways.

I'M DREAMING OF. . .THE BIBLE?

My soul is crushed with a desire for Your Law at all times.
Psalm 119:20

Maybe you know that Psalm 119 is the longest chapter in the Bible. It contains 176 verses! And almost every one of them mentions God's Word, using names like "Your Law."

Several times in Psalm 119, the writer says he loves God's Word. In fact, in verse 20, he says his soul is "crushed with a desire" for it.

Have you ever felt that way about the Bible? If so, great! If not yet, that's okay. The fact is, our interest in and love for God's Word grows as we grow spiritually. Sometimes the Bible can seem confusing, strange, even a little boring. But if you spend time with God's Word—reading it, thinking it over, memorizing parts of it—you'll find that you enjoy it more and more. It begins to make more and more sense. It answers your questions and gives you hope.

And maybe, before long, *you'll* be crushed with a desire for the Bible at all times.

Lord God, please give me a hunger for Your Word. I know it will fill me up.

DON'T BE SAD

"Do not be sad for the joy of the Lord is your strength."
NEHEMIAH 8:10

The story of God's people in the Old Testament is a story of sin, failure, and punishment. Even though God had chosen the Israelites as His special people, they often disobeyed Him—they even worshipped false gods. In time, God allowed the powerful nation of Babylon to punish His people by taking many of them away as "exiles."

But God still loved His people, and many years later some of them returned to their capital city of Jerusalem. As a priest named Ezra read from God's law, the people began to cry. They realized how foolish it was to disobey! But a leader named Nehemiah, who followed God carefully, told them it wasn't a time for weeping. They should eat, drink, and celebrate God's strength.

Ecclesiastes 3:4 says, "There is a time to cry, and a time to laugh; a time to have sorrow, and a time to dance." If you have sinned, be sad and ask God for forgiveness. But once you've confessed your sins, be glad. He forgives—and His joy is your strength.

Lord, make me joyful in Your strength.

LIKE HEZEKIAH

Hezekiah trusted in the Lord, the God of Israel. There was no one like him among all the kings of Judah before him or after him.
2 Kings 18:5

Brave boys do what's right, even if it's hard. Brave boys are leaders.

In the Bible, a young man named Hezekiah was brave. He wanted to honor God, so when he became king, he tore down idols that the people had been worshipping.

The Bible says that Hezekiah "trusted" God. That means he held on to God and never stopped following Him. As Hezekiah obeyed what God told him to do, God was with him. And God is with you too!

Stay close to God and He will be close to you. Look over your life and see if there are any "idols" that need to be torn down. Get rid of the things that distract you from God. Commit to obeying His words. If you do, God will use you to accomplish good things—maybe even great things like Hezekiah did.

Lord, I'm inspired by Hezekiah's story. Help me to be like him by making You my first priority. Help me to stay close to You.

SEE A NEED? FILL A NEED

After we were safe on the island, we knew that it was Malta. The people on the island were very kind to us. It was raining and cold. They made a fire so we could get warm.
ACTS 28:1–2

Here's a simple formula for kindness: See a need? Fill a need.

When the apostle Paul got shipwrecked on the island of Malta, the local people treated him with kindness. They saw he was cold and wet, so they made a fire to warm him up. They gave him a place to stay over the winter. When he was ready to leave, they gave him supplies for his journey. The people saw Paul's needs and filled them.

And Paul took care of the people on Malta. With God's help, he healed the island's sick people, loving them in a very practical way.

Look around today and see what needs you can fill. It doesn't have to be a big thing to be a big blessing to someone.

Lord, may I be a blessing today. Help me to see the needs around me and fill them. I pray You would be honored by my actions.

DON'T BE SHY

"We must tell what we have seen and heard."
Acts 4:20

Can you imagine doing a kind act and being thrown into jail for it? What would you think if God worked a miracle through you, but people got mad instead of excited? That's what happened to Peter and John, two of Jesus' disciples.

Through the power of Jesus' name, they healed a disabled man who worshipped in the temple. But the Jewish religious leaders thought Peter and John were a threat to their power. The leaders told the disciples to be quiet, to stop talking about Jesus. But Peter and John said they could never be silent—they had to tell what they saw and heard about Jesus.

You may never perform a miracle like Peter and John did. But if you follow Jesus, God will do some amazing things for and through you. When He does, be like Peter and John. Say, "I must tell what I have seen and heard!"

Father, I am just an ordinary guy. Please fill me with boldness like Peter and John to do Your work.

CHOOSE LIFE

"I call heaven and earth to speak against you today. I have put in front of you life and death, the good and the curse. So choose life so you and your children after you may live."
DEUTERONOMY 30:19

If the payment for breaking God's law is death, then the reward for following His commands is *life*. And this isn't just some enough-air-to-take-my-next-breath kind of life. This is life that God calls abundant—life that is better than you can imagine.

You might think that the choice between life and death would be simple. *Life, of course!* But in this world many people decide to run away from God. Then, when they die, they're sorry they never took the opportunity to become His friend.

When you follow God, you have the chance to introduce others to real life. Don't keep it to yourself! God's love doesn't stop with you—His great rescue plan is for everyone.

If they hear it, maybe they will choose life too.

Lord, thank You for offering me life—real life. Please help me to share it with everyone I know.

FORGIVE YOUR BROTHER

But Esau ran to meet him and put his arms around him and kissed him.
GENESIS 33:4

Back in Bible times, family members always hugged and kissed each other when they got together. This was especially true if they hadn't seen each other for a long time. But in the story we read in Genesis 33, Jacob was afraid. He had stolen something important from his older brother, Esau. Esau threatened to hurt Jacob, so their mom made him move in with relatives far away.

Years went by. Jacob still was afraid of what Esau might do to him. But when he finally was brave enough to move back home, "Esau ran to meet him" and gave him a warm greeting. Whew! Jacob was so relieved.

Do you have a brother? Even if you don't have a brother at home, every Christian guy is your spiritual brother. If one has done something bad to you, don't even wait for him to come say he's sorry. Tell God that you forgive him and move on.

Lord, it's not easy, but I forgive my brother. Please bring us back together like you did with Jacob and Esau.

TURN FROM SIN

A wise man fears God and turns away from what is sinful, but a fool is full of pride and is not careful.
Proverbs 14:16

Romans 1:29–32 lists a number of sins that Christians should turn away from. It's an ugly list, including things like hating people, jealousy, murder, fighting, lying, gossiping, pride, disobedience toward parents, and not keeping your promises. The Bible tells brave boys (and every follower of Jesus) to stay away from such things. We do because we respect and love God.

But fools aren't careful. They continue to commit these sins, thinking they'll get away with them. But Galatians 6:7–8 says, "Do not be fooled. You cannot fool God. A man will get back whatever he plants! If a man does things to please his sinful old self, his soul will be lost. If a man does things to please the Holy Spirit, he will have life that lasts forever."

Here's an idea: Make a list of things you can do to please the Holy Spirit. Look at the list throughout the day as a reminder. Turn from sin to God.

Lord, I want to please Your Holy Spirit today!

DAY 248

GREAT THINGS HAPPEN WHEN YOU OBEY

The one who keeps looking into God's perfect Law and does not forget it will do what it says and be happy as he does it. God's Word makes men free.
JAMES 1:25

Daniel is a person in the Bible who bravely obeyed God.

He and his friends had been taken far from their own country to serve a distant nation. Because Daniel was wise and hardworking, the kings he worked for trusted him.

But other people were jealous of Daniel, and they tried to get him in trouble. They even tricked the king into throwing Daniel into a pit filled with lions! That must have been scary, but God protected Daniel. When the king got up the next morning, he was amazed to find Daniel still alive.

Daniel told the king that God had sent an angel to shut the mouths of the lions. The king knew that God had helped Daniel, so he made a rule that everyone in his kingdom should worship Daniel's God!

Great things happen when you obey.

Thank You, God, for Daniel. His story gives me courage to be brave and to obey You even when times are tough!

FROM SIN, TO GOD

But you, man of God, turn away from all these sinful things. Work at being right with God. Live a God-like life.
1 Timothy 6:11

Every guy—young boy, teen, or grown man—is tempted to sin. And every guy *does* sin. The problem is disobeying what God tells us to do or not do. For instance, in the verse right before today's scripture, God says we shouldn't love money. Many guys tell themselves, *I don't love money. . .I just like a lot of it.* But that's sin. And it indicates a serious problem deep in the heart.

Some guys say, "Hey, I've never murdered anyone!" But that doesn't make guys good—especially when they disregard what God says and cheat and steal to get more money. We might tell ourselves, *I can think of a whole list of sinful things I don't do.* But there's more to being a Christian than that.

Yes, we need to turn away from sinful things. But we must also "work at being right with God." Start by accepting Jesus, then study and obey God's Word—every part of it.

Lord, help me to turn from sin and to You.

NO GRUMBLING

Men made it very hard for Him and caused Him to suffer, yet He did not open His mouth. He was taken like a lamb to be put to death. A sheep does not make a sound while its wool is cut and He did not open His mouth.
Isaiah 53:7

Brave boys are like Jesus. They don't complain.

If anyone was ever treated unfairly, it was Jesus. He was the perfect man, the one human being who never ever sinned. And yet jealous men arrested Him, beat Him, and hung Him on a cross to die. And what did Jesus say? Not a single word of complaint.

God hates complaining. The Old Testament Israelites often got in trouble for their grumbling. In the New Testament, the apostle Paul wrote, "We must not complain against God as some of them did. That is why they were destroyed" (1 Corinthians 10:10).

Yes, it's easy to complain. Yes, lots of people are doing it. But today, show your love for God by saying *no* to grumbling. Be like Jesus—don't complain!

Lord, it's so easy to grumble and complain. Please help me to recognize and stop it.

FAMILY MATTERS

The mother of Jesus. . .[was] standing near the cross. Mary Magdalene was there also. Jesus saw His mother and the follower whom He loved standing near. He said to His mother, "Woman, look at your son." Then Jesus said to the follower, "Look at your mother." From that time the follower took her to his own house.

John 19:25–27

Members of God's family help each other. When one person is in the hospital, someone else from church might deliver meals when he gets home. God's family helps when someone needs to move, loses a job, or has a baby.

Jesus showed everyone what that kind of care looks like. When He was on the cross, Jesus asked His disciple John to take care of His mother, Mary. Jesus wanted John to treat Mary like his own mother and Mary to treat John like her own son. So John took Mary into his home.

Mary and John were both followers of Jesus. And Jesus made them family.

Lord, You ask me to love people who don't know You. But You also tell me to love my Christian family, showing kindness to people who already love You.

SOUL MATES

*When David had finished speaking to Saul,
the soul of Jonathan became one with the soul
of David. Jonathan loved him as himself.*
1 Samuel 18:1

Jonathan, King Saul's son, could have been jealous when he saw his dad choose David to lead the army into battle. Instead, 1 Samuel 18:4 says, "Jonathan took off his long coat and gave it to David. He gave him his battle-clothes, his sword, his bow and his belt also." In other words, as the king's son, Jonathan could have expected to be named leader of the armies. But out of his love for his friend, Jonathan removed his battle clothes and gave them to David.

To become "one with the soul of" a friend is rare. But when you find such a best friend, you won't hesitate to give up anything for him. You do that because you love your friend like you love yourself. You'd do anything for him without asking questions.

Do you have a friend like this? If not, pray about it. Ask God to send you—and make you—a soul mate.

Father, please send me a friend like Jonathan who will love me as himself.

OKAY, THAT'S SETTLED

Forever, O Lord, Your Word will never change in heaven.
Psalm 119:89

Imagine you're playing football. The other team carries the ball to the 20-yard line and starts celebrating a touchdown. Wouldn't you think, *Hey—that's not right. The rules say you have to cross the goal line to score!*

Every game has rules so that players know what's expected of them. When everyone agrees on how the game is played, they can focus on the actual competition.

God's Word, the Bible, is a rule book for life. It tells us what we're expected to do and how we can "win"—not by defeating other people but by pleasing God. The rules are available for everyone to see, and they don't change. Once you know what God wants, you can live your whole life to make Him happy.

Spend time in God's Word. Learn just what He wants you to do. Be confident that His rules will never change. Knowing what's expected can make you brave.

Okay, that's settled.

Lord God, I thank You for clear rules. Please help me to obey them—to obey You!

NONSTOP PRAYER

Jesus told them a picture-story to show that men should always pray and not give up.
Luke 18:1

Sometimes Jesus taught people through picture-stories, also called parables. In one of these stories, He described a mean, selfish judge and a poor widow—a lady whose husband had died.

The widow went to the judge one day seeking justice. But the judge didn't care—about justice, about the widow, or even about God. Still, though, this lady kept knocking on his door. Finally, because she wouldn't quit asking, the judge decided to help her.

God isn't like that selfish judge—He *wants* to help you. But He also wants you to be like that poor widow, always knocking on His door. As Jesus said, you "should always pray and not give up."

When you need God's help, ask for it. He may answer you right away, or He may make you wait awhile. Either way, keep praying. Like that poor widow, you'll eventually get what you need. God will answer you!

Lord God, please help me not to give up when things get hard. May I be like the woman in Jesus' story, knocking on Your door in nonstop prayer.

HELP MY UNBELIEF

Jesus said to him, "Why do you ask Me that? The one who has faith can do all things."
Mark 9:23

A worried father went to Jesus, seeking help for his son. The boy had an unclean spirit—a demon—that caused him to go stiff and foam at the mouth. The father first asked Jesus' disciples to help, but they couldn't heal the boy. Finally, Jesus got involved.

"If you can do anything to help us," pleaded the father, "take pity on us!"

"Why do you ask Me that?" Jesus replied. "The one who has faith can do all things."

"Lord, I have faith," the father cried. "Help my weak faith to be stronger!" (Mark 9:22–24).

A moment later, the boy was healed.

This man had faith that Jesus could heal his son—but it seems he lacked faith that Jesus was the Son of God.

When you pray for help, is your faith in the fact that God can solve this one problem in your life? Or are you putting your whole life in His hands and trusting Him with all things?

Lord, may I rely on You for everything, not just when I need help in one area.

CHEATERS NEVER WIN

The honor of good people will lead them, but those who hurt others will be destroyed by their own false ways.
PROVERBS 11:3

There's an old saying that goes "Winners never cheat, and cheaters never win." But that doesn't always seem true. Sometimes the cheaters *do* win.

Well, cheaters might win for a while, at least. A golfer can secretly nudge his ball into a better spot. A slick-talking salesman might sell someone a bad car. A weak student might steal answers from a straight-A kid's test. It seems like people get away with cheating all the time.

If you find that frustrating, don't forget that God sees everything. He knows who's honest and who's dishonest, who cheats and who lives with honor. And, in the end, God will make everything right. People who refuse to follow Him and His laws will be punished—they'll "be destroyed by their own false ways." But if you follow Jesus and live to obey Him, there will be rewards.

In the long run, the saying *is* true: Cheaters never win.

Lord God, help me to live with honor—and to pray for those who cheat. You want them to know You too!

MORE IMPORTANT

"Are not two small birds sold for a very small piece of money? And yet not one of the birds falls to the earth without your Father knowing it. God knows how many hairs you have on your head. So do not be afraid. You are more important than many small birds."

MATTHEW 10:29–31

Some people don't think they're worth much. They don't seem to have friends, or get along with others, or do very well in school. It's easy to think less of people like that. *Don't.* God never has. And if you think that way about *yourself*, don't. God never has.

He takes care of little birds. He knows how many hairs grow on your head. Does it seem strange for God to keep track of such things? He does, and here's good news: His Word says "you are more important" than them.

If you don't seem to have friends, you have God. If you don't get along with others, He can help. If you don't do very well in school, He can teach.

Don't be afraid. You are important to God.

Father, thank You for seeing me as important. It means a lot.

GIVING TO THE POOR

He who gives much will be honored,
for he gives some of his food to the poor.
PROVERBS 22:9

For his ninth birthday, Brandon Schulenberg decided he wanted to do something different. He invited twenty-four friends to a party, but he didn't ask them for toys and games. Instead, Brandon suggested they bring grocery items for the local food pantry in his hometown of Murfreesboro, Tennessee. He said his family already had enough stuff, and he didn't want poor people to be hungry.

"I wanted to help people out," Brandon told a local television station. "God told me to do this, so I did. I hope you get to do this too, because it's what God tells us to do."

Brandon's right. When you give to the poor, the scriptures say it's like giving to Jesus (Matthew 25:40). Imagine that! Jesus says He considers it a gift to Himself when you do a kindness for someone in need.

On your next birthday, do you think you could do something brave like Brandon Schulenberg did?

Lord Jesus, I want to help the poor people You love so much. Please give me ideas!

TODAY YOU CAN HELP SOMEONE

"I was hungry and you gave Me food to eat. I was thirsty and you gave Me water to drink. I was a stranger and you gave Me a room. I had no clothes and you gave Me clothes to wear. I was sick and you cared for Me. I was in prison and you came to see Me."

MATTHEW 25:35–36

How often do you see someone in need? Maybe there's a guy standing by the road, holding a cardboard sign that asks for help. Maybe you see homeless people living in tents. In today's Bible passage, Jesus asks you to imagine that each of those people is *Him*.

Maybe that sounds kind of weird. But what if they *were* Jesus? The point is, He wants you to do good things for others. Jesus Himself went around doing a ton of helpful things. One time a boy offered his sack lunch so Jesus could pray over it and use it for others. Jesus prayed all right, then multiplied the bread and fish to feed *thousands* of people!

Lord, You don't ask me to help everyone. But today I will do something simple to help someone.

ON GOOD GROUND

"But those [seeds] which fell on good ground have heard the Word. They keep it in a good and true heart and they keep on giving good grain."
LUKE 8:15

Jesus taught many lessons through parables, a kind of picture-story. Once He described a man scattering seeds. Some fell by the roadside, where people walked on them and birds ate them. Other seeds fell between rocks, but they dried out from lack of water. Some others landed among thorns, which choked out the plants that tried to grow. But a few of the seeds fell on good ground. They grew into healthy plants and created a good harvest—as much as a hundred times more than was planted.

Jesus said that the seed is God's Word. The good ground is people—like you—who hear the Word and let it grow in their hearts. As they follow God's Word and let Him work in their hearts, they produce even more seed—and other people have a chance to know God's Word too.

Keep doing the right thing. Watch how God uses your life to show His love to the world.

Lord, please cause Your Word to grow in my heart.

THE PROVERBS 31 GUY

She opens her hand to the poor,
and holds out her hands to those in need.
Proverbs 31:20

Yeah, this is a verse about a woman—the "Proverbs 31 woman." But we guys can learn a lot from her.

This lady is hardworking. She's confident. And she's generous with other people. Those are good traits for women *and* men, old and young alike.

How can a brave boy open his hand to the poor and hold out his hands to those in need? Some ideas: What about choosing some clothes you don't wear very often and giving them to a homeless shelter? Or maybe sponsoring a poor child through a ministry like Compassion International? How about mowing grass, or shoveling snow, or just spending time with a widow in your neighborhood?

Remember, you don't have to solve every challenge of every needy person. But if you and other brave boys each do a bit, God will multiply your generosity and accomplish amazing things.

Grab some friends and ask them to join you. You could call yourselves the "Proverbs 31 guys"!

Lord, helping the needy is work for everyone—men, women, girls, and boys. Help me to do my part.

BIG PROMISE FROM SAMUEL'S MOM

Then [Hannah] made a promise and said, "O Lord of All, be sure to look on the trouble of Your woman servant, and remember me. Do not forget Your woman servant, but give me a son. If You will, then I will give him to the Lord all his life."

1 Samuel 1:11

The Bible always tells us what really happened. But it doesn't always say, "What happened was good" or "What happened was bad." Most of the time, whether something was good or bad is pretty obvious. But not every time.

How about today's verse? Hannah pleaded with the Lord for a son. Then she promised to give that son back to the Lord.

Now, imagine if *you* were Samuel, the answer to Hannah's prayer. How would you feel about your mom giving you away as soon as you could serve God at the worship center?

It appears that Samuel was happy to live and work in the tabernacle, so this story ends happily. But beware of making big promises that might be tough on other people. Brave boys always live with others in mind.

Lord, make me wise in my decisions and promises.

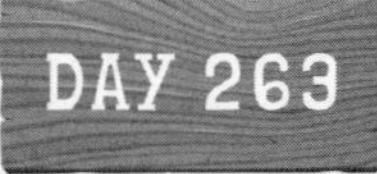

LOVE IS A GREAT GIFT

The man who gives much will have much,
and he who helps others will be helped himself.
PROVERBS 11:25

Blessings are good gifts from a great God. Many of those good gifts come when you obey the gift giver. Loving others is a way you can obey God. He calls love His greatest command.

Share what you have, and God will share with you. It may not be the same thing you shared, but God appreciates the fact that you obeyed Him. Help others, but then don't be surprised when someone helps you just when you need it most. When you show love the way God wants you to, He repays through blessings you might never expect.

Now, don't think you should give just because you want to get something back from God. But when you give, know that blessings come to those who obey.

Love is a great gift, one that can be given and received the same day.

Father, I want You to be pleased with me. May I give and help in Your name to make Your name famous. My friends need to know You.

A COMPLETE REST

And so God's people have a complete rest waiting for them.
Hebrews 4:9

You've probably noticed that your parents are busy. Paying for food, shelter, and clothing for your family is not easy. Running the household isn't easy either. Someone has to clean, shop, plan meals, cook, and organize family activities. At the end of each day, your mom or dad can probably barely keep their eyes open. As you grow older, *your* responsibilities will grow too.

A time is coming, though, when God's people will enjoy a complete rest in heaven. Human bodies won't wear out there. They won't get tired like ours do. Most importantly, we'll never have to fight against our sin nature again.

If you get stressed out about homework or your chores around the house or the temptation to do wrong, be encouraged. Because Jesus died on the cross for sins, He has made it possible for His followers to find a complete rest in heaven one day.

When you're tired and upset, hang in there. Your rest is coming!

Father God, thanks for sending Your only Son to die so I could enjoy eternity with You.

AFTER THE TEST

The man who does not give up when tests come is happy. After the test is over, he will receive the crown of life. God has promised this to those who love Him.

James 1:12

When times are hard, don't give up. Believe that God is working in your life. Hang in there and hold on to His promises.

You can even be *happy* when hard times come. God's Word says that "tests"—the really hard things we go through—help to grow our faith. And faith is what pleases God (Hebrews 11:6). He wants us to wait on Him, to stay faithful, and to keep moving forward. If we do, we can expect a reward. And since God is amazing, His rewards will be too!

God always loves you, and He knows what is best for you. You can trust that He understands and allows whatever is troubling you now. If you stick with God, He'll see you through. So don't give up.

Lord God, You know my struggles. Please give me the faith and strength to stick with You. I believe You'll see me through!

SELFISH DREAMS

You want something you do not have, so you kill.
You want something but cannot get it, so you fight for it.
You do not get things because you do not ask for them.
JAMES 4:2

Brave boys are selfless, not selfish. They look for ways to help and give and share rather than grabbing everything for themselves. They know it's wrong to fight and kill for things they want.

The Bible writer James taught us to ask God for what we want. If our requests are good, God will often give us our desires. But if you ask for things "only to please yourselves" (James 4:3), don't hold your breath waiting for an answer!

Many people think James was one of Jesus' brothers. (Matthew 13:55 mentions four.) Growing up with Jesus, James would have seen the one perfect example of selflessness, day after day after day.

We don't have the same privilege James had. But what he wrote—which God's Holy Spirit will help us remember—is enough for us. We can bypass our selfish dreams and replace them with prayers for truly good things. You know, selfless things.

Father, please give me good things to share.

DAVID AND MEPHIBOSHETH

Then David said, "Is there anyone left of the family of Saul, to whom I may show kindness because of Jonathan?"
2 Samuel 9:1

When a new king takes over, he doesn't want anyone to try to take his job away. Throughout history, many new kings have *killed* anyone who might try to challenge him. Here's why: If the old king has a family member hidden away somewhere, there's a chance that person will come forward and claim to be the rightful king.

When David became king of Israel after Saul, it seemed natural for him to ask if Saul had any children or grandchildren who were still alive. But David wasn't looking to get rid of his competition—he wanted to show *kindness* to Saul's family because Saul's son Jonathan had been David's best friend. When Jonathan's son, Mephibosheth, came forward, David brought him into his palace and treated him like one of his own children.

Even when you think it makes sense to be mean, you can show kindness.

Lord, make me like David. Help me to choose kindness even if it doesn't make sense to the people around me.

HE HEARS

Never stop praying.
1 Thessalonians 5:17

The apostle Paul wrote today's verse hundreds of years after King David lived. But 1 Thessalonians 5:17 really describes David's life.

He wrote about half of the psalms, the biggest book in your Bible. Whether he was excited or scared, happy or sad, David wrote prayer-poems that we still read and sing today. Here's one of them, from a time when he was hiding in a cave from King Saul, who wanted to kill David: "I cry with a loud voice to the Lord. I pray with my voice to the Lord. I talk and complain to Him. I tell Him all my trouble" (Psalm 142:1–2).

Hopefully, we'll never have to run from someone who's trying to take our lives. But there are so many other things in our lives to pray about. David's example, and the apostle Paul's teaching is this: *Never stop praying.*

Whatever is happening in our lives—whether it's good or bad, fun or awful—we can be certain that God hears us when we pray. So pray!

Father, I thank You for hearing my prayers. Help me to turn to You in every situation.

GOOD THINGS

The good that comes from the Lord makes one rich, and He adds no sorrow to it.
PROVERBS 10:22

Have you ever heard of "blessings" and wondered what they are? Some people think a blessing from God must be money, a nice house, or a fancy car. Today's verse uses the word *good* to describe a blessing.

A blessing *is* something good. That could be money, a nice house, or a fancy car. But it could also mean many other things that we sometimes overlook. A good day with your family can be a blessing. So can a cool breeze on a hot day, a warm coat on a cold day, or a good friend and a video game on a rainy day. Blessings include your food, family, and faith.

When you trust God, you can recognize more and more of these good things. Anxiety isn't as strong, fear is replaced by trust, and God's many gifts are seen as *good*.

Lord, I thank You for the things I often overlook, from the warm sunlight to the bed I sleep in. I'm grateful. Help me to see all the good things You do.

DAY 270

EAT THOSE WORDS

Your words were found and I ate them. And Your words became a joy to me and the happiness of my heart.
JEREMIAH 15:16

Ever heard someone say, "I'm going to make you eat those words"? Whoever says that wants to make another person sorry for something they said. For example, a friend might tell you, "You'll never pass that test. It's way too hard!" Your response might be "I'm going to study hard and make you *eat those words*."

But that's not what Jeremiah was talking about in today's verse. He was a prophet, meaning he'd received a special calling to share God's words with the people. Jeremiah *ate those words*—he received them, or took them in—and they filled him with joy and happiness. (Sadly, many who heard those words from Jeremiah were *not* happy—prophets often weren't popular guys.)

How about you? Are you eating those words—the ones in the Bible—every day? Like Jeremiah, are you sharing what you've learned with others? If so, you'll be happy and filled with joy too, no matter how your friends or classmates respond.

Lord, please help me to eat Your words every day.

STILL I TRUST

"Even though He would kill me, yet I will trust in Him."
Job 13:15

Faith is trusting God even though you can't see Him (see Hebrews 11:1). The story of Job teaches us some great lessons about trust.

Job went through the toughest times you could ever imagine. He was a truly good man, but he was attacked by Satan. Job lost his money, his family, and his health—but not the three "friends" who accused him of sinning. It seemed like everyone and everything was against Job.

He was very honest when he talked to God. Sometimes he complained, and one time Job said he wanted to argue with God. But through all of his pain, Job believed in God. And he spoke those incredible words of today's verse: "Even though He would kill me, yet I will trust in Him."

Faith like Job's is believing that no matter how bad your day is, God hasn't left you alone.

God, I thank You for Job's story. Though it's hard to read, it helps me see that You never let go of him—and You'll never let go of me. Please help me to get through my hard days.

AN ANGRY MAN

Do not have anything to do with a man given to anger, or go with a man who has a bad temper. Or you might learn his ways and get yourself into a trap.
PROVERBS 22:24–25

Lots of men set a good example to follow. When you find a guy who's kind or generous or treats everyone respectfully, make an effort to be like him. Or if you find someone who's strong and cool under pressure—you might say, "brave"—you should definitely learn what makes him tick.

Some guys, though, you should avoid like a rattlesnake. One biblical example: an angry man. Mad, bad-tempered men are just trouble—and if you're hanging around with them, you'll probably become like them. That's why the book of Proverbs says "do not have anything to do" with angry people. If you learn their ways, you'll find yourself trapped.

Of course, even with angry people, you should still be kind. But when you find someone whose regular style is mean, harsh, and selfish, don't get too close. There are much better examples to follow.

Lord, may I never be angry all the time. I have so much to be thankful for.

DAY 273

MAKING PEACE

My true helper, I ask you to help these women who have worked with me so much in preaching the Good News to others.
Philippians 4:3

There are many ways to help people. You can rake an older man's leaves, carry a single mom's groceries, or set up a fundraiser for a Christian afterschool program. But some people need help of a different kind.

In Philippians 4, the apostle Paul mentioned two women who were arguing. We don't know what the problem was, but Paul said they needed to "agree as Christians should" (verse 2). And Paul asked a man in their church to step in and help them.

This kind of help is called "peacemaking." Sometimes two people in conflict need a third person to walk them through their problems. The third person needs to be gentle, wise, and kind—they need to know what God's Word says and how to live it out.

Maybe someday that "third person" will be *you*. It takes bravery to help people in conflict, but God gives courage when we ask. And He loves it when we help others to make peace.

Lord, give me courage to help others make peace.

DAY 274

WHAT'S UNFORGIVABLE?

After that [Stephen] fell on his knees and cried out with a loud voice, "Lord, do not hold this sin against them." When he had said this, he died.
Acts 7:60

It's tough to forgive someone who treats you rudely. It's hard to forgive someone who takes something that's important to you. So how hard would it be to forgive someone who is actually *killing* you?

Well, it's impossible—unless God gives you the power.

In Acts 7, a very good man named Stephen was arrested and then killed for teaching about Jesus. And as he was dying, he asked God not to "hold this sin against them." You know that Stephen was a good Christian, because he did exactly what Jesus did when people killed *Him*. "Father, forgive them," Jesus said. "They do not know what they are doing" (Luke 23:34).

In God's eyes, there are no unforgivable sins. And since He tells us to be like Him, we should be willing to forgive anything people do to us. Just remember that what is impossible for humans is completely doable for God. Let Him power your forgiveness.

**Lord, this sounds impossible!
Please help me to forgive others like You do.**

OPTIONS

Elijah came near all the people and said, "How long will you be divided between two ways of thinking? If the Lord is God, follow Him. But if Baal is God, then follow him."
1 Kings 18:21

You know what "options" are? They're like the answers on a multiple-choice test—things you choose from. Sometimes options are similar: *Do I want the red or blue or black bike?* Sometimes they're complete opposites, as we see in the verse above.

Elijah was a prophet of the one true God. He wanted everyone to follow his God rather than the fake gods of the other nations. So he laid out two options for the people to choose from.

They didn't say anything at first. But after Elijah prayed and God sent fire from heaven, the people knew that the Lord was God. The choice was clear.

God gives you the option to follow Him too. He might not send you fire from heaven, but He has given you the Bible and Christian friends and all of creation to point you to Him.

If the Lord is God, follow Him.

**Lord, I believe You are God.
Help me to follow You every day!**

ROCK BOTTOM

"You have trusted in your own strength and in your many soldiers. The noise of battle will rise up among your people. All your strong cities will be destroyed."
Hosea 10:13–14

You may have heard someone talk about another person hitting "rock bottom." The phrase describes someone who's failed so many times that he can't go any lower. Often times the guy at rock bottom got there because he made poor choices—he thought he knew what he was doing, but he found out he was very wrong.

People often trust their own ability, strength, skill, money—even the leaders and soldiers of their country—before they trust God. Make sure you're not one of those people!

God gives His children certain abilities and skills, which He wants us to use for building His kingdom. But we should never think that those God-given talents and opportunities make us special or that they allow us to move forward without God. If we act like that, we'll make the same mistake Israel made in Hosea 10—before they hit rock bottom.

See that example and run the other way!

Lord, I don't want to trust my own strength. I want to trust You.

SMALL GUY, BIG GOD

We will receive from Him whatever we ask if we obey Him and do what He wants.

1 John 3:22

You probably know the story of David and Goliath. David was a young guy carrying food to his older brothers in Israel's army. Goliath was a gigantic warrior of the enemy Philistines.

When David heard Goliath making fun of God, he was upset. And when none of the older, stronger soldiers would stand up to Goliath, David said *he* would.

Later in life, David wrote many beautiful prayers in the Psalms. Can't you just imagine the young David praying for God's help and protection as he stepped up to face the insulting Goliath?

David entered the fight with a simple sling and five small stones, though he only needed one to knock out the giant.

When you're doing what God tells you to do, He will answer your prayers for help. Goliath was a mighty soldier, but he didn't stand a chance against a small guy with a big God.

God, I want to be like David and stick up for You. Please help me to become a brave boy who shows people how great You are!

EAT WELL

"He let you be hungry which helped you to not have pride. Then He fed you with bread from heaven which you and your fathers had not known. He did this to make you understand that man does not live by bread alone. But man lives by everything that comes out of the mouth of the Lord."

DEUTERONOMY 8:3

Some of us, given the chance, would eat junk food all the time. Cotton candy, chocolate bars, potato chips—the junkier the better, right?

But then Mom or Dad or your teacher steps in to say, "Hey, you need to eat some real food!" Grilled chicken, fruit salad, string cheese—something that's better for your body.

Our spirits have a similar need. We can fill up with video games, movies, and music, but our "real food" is God's Word. In fact, the Bible says that's what we truly live on—"everything that comes out of the mouth of the Lord."

Sometimes when you're sad or lonely or upset, it just means your spirit is hungry. Fill it up with the Bible.

Heavenly Father, I want both my body and spirit to be healthy. Please help me to "eat well."

BELIEVING WITHOUT SEEING

Jesus said to the captain, "Go your way.
It is done for you even as you had faith to believe."
The servant was healed at that time.
MATTHEW 8:13

While He was on earth, Jesus healed a lot of people. Some were healed by His touch. Others were healed by His words. Those people who were healed believed Jesus was the Son of God because they saw the evidence.

When an officer in the Roman army heard Jesus was nearby, he asked the healer to help one of his servants. Jesus offered to go to the soldier's home, but the officer stopped him. He believed Jesus could heal the sick servant without making the long walk to be with him. The officer didn't even need to see the healed servant to believe that Jesus had done a miracle.

Trusting Jesus means knowing He is capable of miracles, even when you can't see them happening. Faith is actually believing what you *cannot* see. Are you trusting God in that way? If not, ask Him for more faith—and "see" what He does for you!

Lord, help me to believe in You when I can't see what You are doing.

MAKE KNOWN, BE KNOWN

"Whoever makes Me known in front of men,
I will make him known to My Father in heaven."
MATTHEW 10:32

Do you know what it means to be ashamed? That's feeling embarrassed by something about yourself, or something you've done, or something you're connected to—like Jesus. Many people in the world hate Jesus, and they'll make things hard on those of us who follow Him.

But Jesus wants us to be brave, not ashamed. He wants us to tell people in our life about His life, death, and resurrection. His "Great Commission" tells us to teach others about the good news of God's grace.

Those who don't know Jesus may act like you're crazy for talking about Him. They might call you names or treat you badly. But Jesus has promised us, "I am with you always, even to the end of the world" (Matthew 28:20). Since He is the all-powerful God, He can give us the strength to do whatever He tells us to.

When we help other people to know Jesus, He makes sure God the Father knows *us*. That's a reason to speak out!

Father, help me to be bold when I speak of Jesus.

UNFAIR

"Do not be troubled or angry with yourselves because you sold me here. For God sent me before you to save your life."
GENESIS 45:5

If there had been a "Worst Brothers of the Year Award," Joseph's brothers would have won.

Joseph was dad's favorite son. And his brothers *hated* that. But they didn't just pick on Joseph—they actually sold their younger brother as a slave. Then the older brothers agreed to trick their dad into believing that a wild animal had killed Joseph.

This may sound crazy, but it's true: God took the bad behavior of those ten older brothers and used it for good. The evil they did to Joseph actually saved many lives!

It may seem unfair to have to put up with cruel brothers. But if you've ever had a tough experience with a sibling, know this: Your future isn't decided by the things anyone else does to you.

Be like Joseph. Know that God is in every situation, and look for what He's doing. Even when life seems unfair, trust Him.

Lord, I don't always understand why things happen to me. But I will trust that You can use my hurt to help others.

BE UNASHAMED

Onesiphorus was not ashamed of me in prison. He came often to comfort me. May the Lord show loving-kindness to his family.
2 Timothy 1:16

The apostle Paul was in prison in Rome when he wrote his second letter to Timothy. Paul was often jailed for preaching the gospel, and some people believe he was near the end of his life as he wrote the verse above. Sadly, many Christians in the area had deserted Paul—they were embarrassed that he was in prison for Jesus. But one person was different: Onesiphorus.

Okay, so we can all be glad that our parents didn't give us such a long, tricky name. But we can also learn a lot from Mr. O. He was not ashamed of Paul, he "came often to comfort" Paul, and he made a big difference in the apostle's tough life.

Do you have a friend at school or in the neighborhood who gets picked on for talking about Jesus? This is your chance to be an Onesiphorus. Don't leave your friend to suffer alone. Find him. Encourage him. Make a big difference in his life.

Lord, give me the courage to stand up for my Christian friends.

ASK, ASK, ASK

"I say to you, he may not get up and give him bread because he is a friend. Yet, if he keeps on asking, he will get up and give him as much as he needs."
LUKE 11:8

Jesus told a story about two friends. One guy asked his buddy for some bread. Nothing too crazy about that, right? Except it was the middle of the night and the second guy didn't want to get out of bed. But the first friend kept asking. He just didn't stop. And, finally, the second guy got up and gave his buddy as much as he needed.

Jesus finished that story by saying that we—as God's children—should ask in the same way. We should ask, ask, ask.

Prayer is important to Jesus. He wants us to talk to God through Him. And even when we don't get exactly what we pray for exactly when we want it, we should keep praying. Don't doubt God's promises or His goodness. Just keep asking—that nighttime bread is coming!

Teach me, Lord, to be faithful in prayer. Please help me to understand Your will for my life.

KEEP LOVING JESUS!

"We must keep on doing the work of Him Who sent Me while it is day. Night is coming when no man can work."
JOHN 9:4

Why do boys and girls love Jesus? In the Gospels, it's clear that they loved Jesus because He loved them first. Jesus wasn't posing for artists when He invited kids to gather around. He didn't have to do any coaxing—children loved Him. So did their parents, who were eager for Jesus to bless their kids.

Like a beloved uncle or grandfather, Jesus put His hands on the kids' heads and prayed for them. You can just imagine parents reminding their children, "Do you remember when Jesus prayed for you?" What a wonderful memory that would be.

Some people say that adults who love children are really just kids themselves at heart. That is, they're people who've held on to the best qualities of childhood—including loving Jesus.

So loving Jesus isn't just for boys. It's for young men, middle-aged men, and old men as well. You could say that loving Jesus is the most important thing you can do in your whole life.

Lord God, I want to keep loving Jesus!

IT JUST MAKES SENSE

O Lord, be kind to us. We have waited for You. Be our strength every morning. Save us in the time of trouble.
Isaiah 33:2

When you need help, who do you go to? A total stranger or a good friend?

Of course you go to someone you already know. Somebody you've spent time with. Someone you can talk to and be honest with.

When you need the help that God can give, it just makes sense that He's more ready to help people who already know Him. People who have spent time with Him, talked with Him, waited for Him. That's what the prophet Isaiah was saying in today's verse. When we've already "waited" for God, we can confidently ask Him for things—to be our strength, to save us from trouble.

We can be brave in approaching God when we've already been His friend. And Jesus told us exactly how to be that kind of friend: "You are My friends if you do what I tell you" (John 15:14).

It just makes sense.

Lord God, I want to be Your friend. Help me to obey You then to bravely ask You for help.

CHOOSING LAST PLACE

"Whoever wants to be first among you, must be the one who is owned and cares for all."
Mark 10:44

Right before guys play basketball at recess, the two captains start picking players for their teams. Everyone gulps. Okay, maybe not everyone—but some guys are secretly thinking, *I hope I'm not picked last.* That's never fun, is it?

Actually, it can be.

Look again at today's Bible verse. Jesus is talking to His closest friends, and He basically says, "Quit worrying about who I'm going to pick to be captains. Instead, you should be willing to sit on the bench. Be willing to fetch towels when the other guys come off the court. Serve them and you'll be the *real* captain on My team."

The weird thing? It works. Even though you're doing the grunt work, you really do feel like the top dog.

Every time you line up to play ball or divide into teams for a school project, remember what Jesus said. Serve the other guys (or girls) on your team. Then imagine Jesus watching and cheering for you!

Lord, I believe You. I'm going to choose to serve other people.

RESPECT

When I saw Him, I fell down at His feet like a dead man. He laid His right hand on me and said, "Do not be afraid. I am the First and the Last. I am the Living One. I was dead, but look, I am alive forever. I have power over death and hell."

REVELATION 1:17–18

John wrote the book of Revelation. He was also a disciple of Jesus. John, "the disciple Jesus loved," was a personal friend of God's Son.

God allowed John to see into heaven. He saw his friend Jesus again. But this time Jesus looked different. John was so frightened that he dropped to the floor.

John was overwhelmed because Jesus was so much more than just a friend. He was actually God! But look what Jesus told John: "Do not be afraid."

You don't need to fear Jesus. But you should show Him respect. Why? Because He loved you enough to pay the price that God the Father placed on sin. Jesus died to take your punishment, then rose from the dead and returned to heaven.

He loved. We respect.

God, thank You for Jesus. I respect His love and sacrifice for me.

THE GIFT OF SHARING

If someone has the gift of sharing what he has, he should give from a willing heart.
Romans 12:8

The twelfth chapter of Romans lists many "spiritual gifts"—special abilities that God gives to His children. One of these gifts is sharing what we have. The verse may be talking about giving to the church, or it might include giving to anyone who has a need. People with the gift of sharing are always looking for ways to give. They can't wait to do it!

Not everybody has the spiritual gift of sharing—but everybody can and should share. If you're a child of God, sharing should be part of who you are. God saw your need, and He reached out to give Jesus. Now He expects you to "pay it forward" by reaching out to others.

When you see people in need, do you think to share with them right away? If so, maybe that's your spiritual gift. If not, think about Romans 12:8 and ask God to give you a willing heart. He'll be happy to answer that prayer!

God, give me a willing heart to share with others. I want to be like You!

LIKE A TREE ON A RIVERBANK

Happy is the man who does not walk in the way sinful men tell him to, or stand in the path of sinners, or sit with those who laugh at the truth. But he finds joy in the Law of the Lord and thinks about His Law day and night.

Psalm 1:1–2

Some things in the Bible are very plain—like the formula for happiness in Psalm 1:1–2.

There are three things to avoid, and one to pursue. The "stay aways" first: Don't befriend people who always make bad choices. Don't walk where they're going, don't stop to hang out with them, and definitely don't sit down to stay. Don't hang out with people who "laugh at the truth"—that is, God and His Word—because they're trouble. They won't bring you happiness.

What will? Well, God and His Word. Make your quiet time a top priority. Read your Bible and pray. When you take the time to listen to what God's saying, then think about it "day and night," you'll be happy. You'll be like a strong, healthy tree on a riverbank (Psalm 1:3).

Lord, may I choose my friends wisely—and always spend time with You.

MIRACLES FOR YOUR FAMILY

He has remembered His agreement forever, the promise He made to last through a thousand families-to-come.
Psalm 105:8

How good that you have access to God's Word, the Bible. It's even better when you believe God's promises, obey His commands, and enjoy His rich blessings. Those blessings include miracles—incredible things God does for His beloved children.

Over the years, how many miracles has God done for you and your family? If you're not sure, make a list. Ask your dad or mom to help you recognize miracles that God has done for you. Maybe call your grandparents for help. Try to come up with at least four miracles your family has received from God.

Here are some examples: Has God saved anyone's life? Has He healed someone? Has He provided money right when your family needed it? Did He provide just the right house at the right time?

Of course, there are many other kinds of miracles too. Figure out what they are, and then say, "Thanks, God!"

Lord, You do millions of miracles every day, all around the world. Help me to recognize the miracles You have done for me and my family.

GOD WORKS THROUGH US

O Lord, You will give us peace,
for You have done all our works for us.
Isaiah 26:12

Some things in life are hard to understand. But that doesn't mean they're not true.

Here's a mystery for you: When you do good things, it's really *God* doing them. He's the one who gives you the desire and ability to say no to bad things and yes to His own plans. That's what Isaiah was saying in today's verse. It's what the apostle Paul meant when he wrote, "He is working in you. God is helping you obey Him. God is doing what He wants done in you" (Philippians 2:13).

When you dream of doing great things, that's really God's dream. Not a dream to make a million dollars—that's nothing to the God who made (and owns) the whole universe. But dreams of helping people, encouraging people, pointing people to God through His Son, Jesus Christ—now those are the dreams that excite God. And when He passes the dream on to you, you'll be excited too!

Let God live His dreams through you.

Lord, please use me to accomplish Your plans in this world.

A PURE MIND

Christian brothers, keep your minds thinking about whatever is true, whatever is respected, whatever is right, whatever is pure, whatever can be loved, and whatever is well thought of. If there is anything good and worth giving thanks for, think about these things.

PHILIPPIANS 4:8

Have you heard the phrase "You are what you eat"? It means that if you eat healthy foods, you'll be healthier—and if you eat unhealthy foods, you end up hurting yourself. That is true not just of foods but of what we put into our hearts and minds too.

The apostle Paul said that if we spend time thinking of bad things, we'll become bad. That's why he said to focus on what is true, respectable, right, pure, lovely, and "well thought of." It's why the book of Proverbs says, "Keep your heart pure for out of it are the important things of life" (4:23).

A great way to do this is to memorize scripture. Get God's Word into your heart and mind and think about it throughout the day. That will keep your mind pure—and your whole self healthy.

Father, help me to store good, truthful thoughts in my mind.

SHARE WHAT YOU HAVE

[John the Baptist] answered them, "If you have two coats, give one to him who has none. If you have food, you must share some."
LUKE 3:11

True story: Maria, who lived on the corner of Fourteenth and Haynes, was nearing her one hundredth birthday. Next door was a boy named Allen. His mom sent him to Maria's place every night with a plate of food. This very old lady shared the same food as Allen every night, and the two became friends.

What John the Baptist said to do in Luke 3:11 is what Allen's family did. They had food, and they shared it. John also said that if you have two coats and know someone who is cold, hand one over. Jesus—who was John's relative and Lord—calls that love.

And the giving doesn't have to stop with food or clothes. What ideas can you come up with to show love using something you already have? Love shares what it has.

Lord, help me to be generous with what I have. It's easy to think that if I give, I won't have, but Your giving to me never runs out.

FUTURE HOPE

"'For I know the plans I have for you,' says the Lord, 'plans for well-being and not for trouble, to give you a future and a hope.'"
JEREMIAH 29:11

This verse was a promise to God's people who'd seen an enemy overrun their nation. They'd been forced to leave Jerusalem and move to Babylon. Jeremiah 29:10 says they needed to stay there seventy years before God brought them back home.

Seventy years is a long time. Most of these people wouldn't live long enough to see God's promise fulfilled—so until that time, He told them to build houses, get married, have children—and work to make Babylon better.

That took courage. God's people were starting over in a new place. They were supposed to act like it was home, knowing that one day—far in the future—God would bring their kids and grandkids and great-grandkids back to their real home.

God is always faithful but never in a hurry. If you're in a hard time, He might not change it anytime soon. But He'll always be right there with you.

Lord, thank You for walking through hard times with me. You give me hope for the future.

WHEN YOU'RE WEAK

He answered me, "I am all you need.
I give you My loving-favor. My power works best
in weak people." I am happy to be weak and have
troubles so I can have Christ's power in me.
2 CORINTHIANS 12:9

Few people have served God like the apostle Paul did. He was so committed to Jesus that the Lord once gave him a special dream. Paul actually got to see into heaven!

That might make a guy feel pretty special. But to keep Paul from becoming boastful, God also gave him a "thorn in [the] flesh" (2 Corinthians 12:7 NIV)—some trouble that reminded him to be humble.

Paul asked God several times to take the trouble away. But God said no. Why? Because *God* was all Paul needed! God told Paul that His power works best in people who feel weak. Have you ever felt weak? God uses those times as a reminder that He is with us. He will give you strength when you just don't have power of your own.

Paul began to see his bad days as opportunities to feel God's power. And so can you!

Lord, please help me to see problems the way Paul did.

A BOY'S FAITH

"And you must love the Lord your God with all your heart and with all your soul and with all your strength."
DEUTERONOMY 6:5

Some people act like a boy's belief in God doesn't count. But the apostle Paul said to Timothy, "Hold on to what you have learned and know to be true. Remember where you learned them. You have known the Holy Writings *since you were a child*. They are able to give you wisdom that leads to being saved from the punishment of sin by putting your trust in Christ Jesus" (2 Timothy 3:14–15, italics added).

True, you can't understand everything you hear and read in the Bible right now. So? There's nothing wrong with having to learn more about God and the Christian faith. After all, 1 Corinthians 13:11 says, "When I was a child, I spoke like a child. I thought like a child. I understood like a child." In other words, the Bible doesn't criticize a boy's knowledge and way of thinking. Just keep learning and growing!

Lord, I believe everything that I know of the Bible right now. But please keep teaching me!

DON'T IGNORE YOUR GIFTS

We all have different gifts that God has given to us by His loving-favor. We are to use them.
ROMANS 12:6

What would you love to get next Christmas? A new video game system? A dirt bike? Tickets to a huge sporting event?

Imagine that on Christmas morning you found the one thing you wanted, tagged with your name. Cool! Then you walked away and never used it.

What? Get a great gift only to ignore it? Never to enjoy it yourself or allow the gift giver to see you using it? That's crazy.

When you become a Christian, God gives you "spiritual gifts," special abilities you can use to bless others. They include teaching, giving, leadership, and "discernment"—helping people to understand the right things. But you've got to *use* your gift to please God and help others.

Sure, you're still young. But if you sense that God has given you a certain gift, look for ways to use it. Talk to your parents or your pastor and see if there's a place for you to serve. Don't ignore your gifts!

Father God, show me my gifts—then help me use them to please You and help others.

LIVE LIKE KING DAVID

"As for you, walk before Me as your father David walked, with a true heart doing what is right."
1 Kings 9:4

It would be great if you could live a perfect and sinless life. But God knows the truth—you're going to sin sometimes. You're occasionally going to disobey the Lord. When you do, it's important to admit your sin and turn back to God. That's what King David did.

Imagine your name is David and you're reading the Bible for the first time. When you get to the David and Goliath story, you'll cheer. Then when you get to the David and Bathsheba story, you'll cringe. Yes, King David broke half of the Ten Commandments when he stole another man's wife and then had that man killed. That was *very* bad. But when David admitted his own sinfulness and turned away from evil, God forgave him and welcomed him back. That's why people still remember David as a good king.

When you sin, what will happen? You have a choice.

Lord, when I fail, please help me to stop, pray, admit my sin, and start living for You again.

GUARD AND DEFEND

Do not worry. Learn to pray about everything. Give thanks to God as you ask Him for what you need. The peace of God is much greater than the human mind can understand. This peace will keep your hearts and minds through Christ Jesus.

PHILIPPIANS 4:6–7

God gave you a command: "Do not worry." That's hard to do. A lot of things can go wrong in life, right? But if you worry, you can't rest. You might feel hopeless. And you won't be grateful.

God has a plan for avoiding worry: You need to pray! Talk to God about your concerns, and don't leave anything out. Tell Him "thank You" before He even answers your prayer. Before long, you'll find yourself feeling *peace*.

When you have peace in your life, worry isn't making your world crazy. Peace stands like a soldier outside your heart, guarding what you feel and defending what you think.

We can't understand how it all works, but it does work. God promised peace, and Jesus provides it.

Lord, You don't just suggest that I stop worrying— You tell me to stop. I ask You to send Your peace into my heart and mind.

EATING AND DRINKING

This is what I have seen to be good and right: to eat and to drink and be happy in all the work one does under the sun during the few years of his life which God has given him. For this is his reward.
Ecclesiastes 5:18

The Bible talks a lot about eating and drinking. And why not? God created food and drinks for us to enjoy. He also put us into families, where we can learn and grow as we're protected from the world around us. When food and family come together, the message of Ecclesiastes 5:18 is true: It's "good and right," a happy reward from God.

But, if you're like a lot of boys, you might prefer to do other things than sit down to a family meal. Hey, there are bikes to ride, hoops to shoot, videos to watch, right? Who wants to hit the brakes for a half hour around the dinner table?

Don't rush through your family dinner. If you do, you're missing one of God's intended gifts. Take your time over food and drink with your family. It's good and right—a reward, even!

Lord, may I enjoy my family mealtime.

NO SHAME

O my God, I trust in You. Do not let me be ashamed.
Do not let those who fight against me win.
PSALM 25:2

Does it ever feel like it's crazy to be good? Like being kind, honest, and helpful doesn't get you anywhere? Like bad people usually win?

People have felt that way for thousands of years. King David, who wrote many of the psalms, asked God to keep the bad guys from winning. David prayed that he wouldn't be ashamed—he wanted to see that doing right paid off. That following God was really the best way to go.

We don't know why, but God does allow evil in this world. Sometimes bad people seem to get ahead. Living as a Christian is tough.

But none of that should take away our trust in God. The Bible says He is good, He is in control, and He has His own reasons for allowing tough things—reasons we just can't understand. But we can still trust Him. He will not let us be ashamed. And, whether now or in eternity, those who fight against us will not win.

Lord, help me to trust in You.
Do not let me be ashamed.

BREAKING THE RULES

Then the daughter of Pharaoh came to wash herself in the Nile. Her young women walked beside the Nile. She saw the basket in the tall grass and sent the woman who served her to get it. She opened it and saw the child. The boy was crying. She had pity on him and said, "This is one of the Hebrews' children."

EXODUS 2:5–6

While they were in Egypt, the people of Israel grew in number. And that made the Egyptians nervous. Finally, Pharaoh decided the Israelites should never get powerful enough to rebel against him. So he ordered that all their male babies should be killed.

Moses' mom disobeyed the order, keeping her baby alive by putting him in a floating basket in the river. Pharaoh's daughter disobeyed the order and adopted Moses as her son. Both women knew that murdering babies was wrong.

God used these rule-breaking women to free the Israelites from slavery. If you ever find human rules that go against God's teaching, you can break them. God will bless you for following Him.

Lord, please give me the wisdom and boldness to follow Your rules instead of man's.

GOD KNOWS

"For I the Lord will speak, and whatever I say will be done."
EZEKIEL 12:25

Can you tell the future? Oh, you can guess what might happen tomorrow or next year, but you can't say anything for sure.

God can though. That's because He knows everything, and He has all power.

In today's verse, God was talking to a man named Ezekiel. He was a prophet, a person who spoke for God, telling other people just what God had told him. Ezekiel told the people some hard times were coming, but they didn't believe him. So God said, "Whatever I say *will be done*." And it was.

When God says He'll do something, you can trust that He'll keep that promise. When He says that He will be with you (Hebrews 13:5), protect you (2 Thessalonians 3:3), and someday take you to heaven (John 14:3), you can believe it all—and live your life with courage.

God knows the future. God knows *your* future. And God has the power to keep you safe in His care.

Heavenly Father, I'm glad you know all things. Please make me brave to follow You into my future.

ALWAYS GOOD TO PRAY

Is anyone among you suffering? He should pray.
Is anyone happy? He should sing songs of thanks to God.
James 5:13

The definition of prayer is really simple: It is communicating with God. You can pray by singing songs to Him or asking Him for help or even talking to Him like a best friend, discussing your day at school or something that's happening at home.

Praying is not reserved for special occasions. In fact, the apostle Paul wrote that Christians should "never stop praying" (1 Thessalonians 5:17). Paul prayed when he was away from the friends he loved, when he was shipwrecked in the open ocean, and many times when he'd been arrested for sharing his faith. He had numerous opportunities to pray, and he took them!

Our heavenly Father doesn't expect us to be in a good mood in order to pray. He doesn't demand that we use special words. He doesn't care if we're sad or grouchy or afraid. He just wants us to talk to Him. It is always good to pray!

Father God, please help me to become a man of prayer. I want to know You as my best friend.

TWO BOSSES

"No servant can have two bosses. He will hate the one and love the other. Or, he will be faithful to one and not faithful to the other. You cannot be faithful to God and to riches at the same time."

LUKE 16:13

You might know someone who has two jobs. Maybe they work weekdays in a store then help at a restaurant over the weekend. If some people have "two bosses," does that mean today's verse is wrong?

No. Jesus wasn't really talking about jobs here. He was saying that people must choose the most important thing in life. Will that be God or something else?

Many people think "riches"—money—is the most important thing in life. And they work very hard to get more and more of it. But Jesus also said, "What does a man have if he gets all the world and loses or gives up his life?" (Luke 9:25).

It's okay to work hard and enjoy what you own. But remember that when you follow God, you must choose Him first, every time.

Lord, I don't want anything in my life to be more important than You. May I follow You with all my heart.

GOD IS MY SONG

"See, God saves me. I will trust and not be afraid. For the Lord God is my strength and song. And He has become the One Who saves me."
Isaiah 12:2

So, how's your voice? Could you appear on one of those TV singing contests, or are you the kind of guy who can't carry a tune in a bucket?

The Bible tells Christians to sing—no matter how good or bad your voice might be. "Sing the Songs of David and the church songs and the songs of heaven with hearts full of thanks to God" (Colossians 3:16). The first part of that verse explains why: "Let the teaching of Christ and His words keep on living in you. These make your lives rich and full of wisdom. Keep on teaching and helping each other."

Songs about God help our hearts to focus on Him—to remember how He's saved us and given us strength. We sing because we're happy for all He's done for us. And as we sing, we find that God takes away our fears. Trust. Don't be afraid. Make God your song.

Father, give me a song of praise to You.

OBEY RIGHT AWAY

"Whoever hears these words of Mine and does them, will be like a wise man who built his house on rock. The rain came down. The water came up. The wind blew and hit the house. The house did not fall because it was built on rock."

MATTHEW 7:24–25

Sometimes it's hard to do what God says. You might read something in your Bible and think, *There's no way I can do that.* But with God, there's always a way.

A man named Abraham had to do something really hard. He had lived in the same place for a long time. He was part of a larger family, and he was comfortable with life. But that's when God told him to pack up and move a long way away. Everything was going to change!

Abraham didn't come up with a million reasons *not* to do what God said. He just obeyed.

What is God telling you to do? Maybe He wants you to befriend the new kid at school. Maybe you need to treat your parents better. Whatever God tells you, be brave and obey right away!

God, please help me to be like Abraham and do what You say immediately.

DAY 308

INSTANT AND FULL FORGIVENESS

He has not punished us enough for all our sins. He has not paid us back for all our wrong-doings. . . . He has taken our sins from us as far as the east is from the west.

Psalm 103:10, 12

The Bible says that fathers need to discipline their sons. But it also teaches that sons can do some really terrible things. Sometimes, "proportional discipline" isn't possible. You know, "You're grounded for life" doesn't really work.

Sean's dad prayed for wisdom and decided he should offer instant and full forgiveness. In fact, he made a promise to Sean that he would always do that. That way Sean knew that even when he confessed really bad behavior to his dad, he would still find deep love, along with immediate and complete forgiveness.

Of course, bad behavior still brings consequences, so it's always best to do the right thing. But if you do wrong, maybe your parent will be like Sean's dad. Even if not, you have a heavenly Father who offers instant and full forgiveness to those who ask.

Lord God, give me the courage to admit when I've done wrong—I want Your complete forgiveness!

GIVE GOD TIME

I did not give up waiting for the Lord.
And He turned to me and heard my cry.
Psalm 40:1

You remember Job's story, right? He went through a *lot* of pain and suffering even though he hadn't done anything to cause it. In one day, Job lost all of his possessions as well as all ten of his children. And then, soon afterward, he lost his health. Soon even his wife and friends turned against him.

Through all of his hurt, Job never gave up his faith in God. He "did not give up waiting for the Lord," as today's verse says, and God blessed him. In fact, God gave Job's belongings back two times over. And God gave Job another ten kids and a very long life.

What's the point for us? That God is full of tenderness and mercy! In our worst times or our most awesome times, He wants us to call out to Him. Yes, Job suffered a lot—but he was patient to wait for God. When God responded, He did it in a big way.

Dear God, you are a good Father.
Give me strength to wait on Your blessings.

FORGIVE AND HELP

Now the Syrians had gone out in groups of soldiers, and had taken a little girl from the land of Israel. She served Naaman's wife. And she said to her owner, "I wish that my owner's husband were with the man of God who is in Samaria! Then he would heal his bad skin disease."

2 Kings 5:2–3

Too many TV shows and movies are based on revenge. The main characters seem to believe, *If you do something bad to me, I'll do something worse to you.*

That's exactly the opposite of what Jesus taught. He said, "If you have anything against anyone, forgive him" (Mark 11:25). Today's verse is an amazing example of that.

A young girl from Israel was kidnapped by soldiers from Syria. Then she was forced to serve in the Syrian commander's house. If this girl was in a modern movie, she'd probably poison his food—but she didn't do anything like that. Instead, she gave the commander some very good advice: Find the prophet Elisha and be healed.

The world says, "Fight back." Brave boys follow God's command to forgive and help.

Father, give me Your strength to forgive and help—every time.

DON'T BE MAD

Then [Joseph] sent his brothers away. As they left he said to them, "Do not be mad at each other on the way."
GENESIS 45:24

If you want to know what forgiveness looks like, this is a great example.

Joseph had been sold into slavery by his brothers. But over many years, God worked a miracle: Joseph became a ruler in his new home of Egypt.

Then came a famine. There was no rain. Crops didn't grow. People began to starve. But God had made Joseph very wise, and he was prepared. Joseph had saved back enough food to save many lives.

His brothers came to Egypt, hoping to buy food. They had to meet with Joseph, but they had no idea this was the brother they had treated so badly.

Joseph, though, recognized his brothers—and *he forgave them*. Then he said something they probably never expected: "Do not be mad at each other." Joseph's brothers expected anger, but Joseph was kind.

Life is always better when you choose to forgive.

God, please help me choose to be kind, to forgive, to love. Give me courage to choose Your way, even when it's hard.

STANDING FOR JESUS

Many women were looking on from far away. These had followed Jesus from the country of Galilee. They had cared for Him.
MATTHEW 27:55

In the movie version of *The Chronicles of Narnia*, Susan and Lucy look sadly at Aslan's dead body on a stone table. But as they walk away, the stone table splits in two. Aslan comes back to life and tells the girls that death has been turned backward.

Susan and Lucy are like the many women who cared for Jesus during His life on earth. Women such as Mary Magdalene and another Mary, the mother of James and Joseph, as well as Zebedee's wife, the mom of Jesus' disciples James and John. These women were with Jesus shortly before He was killed, and they stuck around afterward, when Jesus' male friends all ran away. Today we still talk about the courage of these female followers.

Do you have the courage to stand up for Jesus? If you do, the world won't always be happy about it. But Jesus will certainly notice.

Father God, I want to be remembered as someone who stood up for Jesus and His followers.

CHANGE OF PLANS

Joseph awoke from his sleep. He did what the angel of the Lord told him to do. He took Mary as his wife.
MATTHEW 1:24

There's a story in the Bible about a man who decided to break a commitment. Then God got hold of him and changed his mind. He did what he was originally planning to do—and he was blessed.

The man was Joseph, and his commitment was to become the husband of Mary. That's the Mary who was pregnant with Jesus—but because Joseph knew he wasn't the father, he thought he should walk away from the marriage.

God, though, sent an angel to tell Joseph to do what he'd promised. Mary was pregnant through a miracle, and God wanted Joseph to be her husband—and to help raise her boy, who was actually the Son of God!

Joseph obeyed. He trusted that God would work everything out. And two thousand years later we remember him as the husband of Mary and the "father" of Jesus.

Today, what might God be telling *you* to do?

Lord, please show me what You want me to do and give me the strength to do it.

MAKING GOD HAPPY

A man cannot please God unless he has faith. Anyone who comes to God must believe that He is. That one must also know that God gives what is promised to the one who keeps on looking for Him.
HEBREWS 11:6

If you have a friend who doubts everything you say, that's not much of a friendship. Friends trust each other. When one person betrays your trust or doesn't believe in you, the happiness from that friendship will quickly disappear.

God is much better than a friend, but the same rules apply. When you doubt the things God says, the relationship suffers. When you act in ways that only make you happy, God isn't pleased. If you really trusted Him, you'd know that following His rules keeps you safe.

Do you want to make God happy? Then don't question His goodness, even when life seems hard. Believe His plans are the best. Choose to live for Him instead of yourself.

That's all part of faith. And faith is what makes God happy.

Lord, I want to make You happy. Help me to believe Your promises more and more.

KEEP GOING!

"God has helped me. To this day I have told these things to the people who are well-known and to those not known."
ACTS 26:22

For traveling all through the world telling people about Jesus, the apostle Paul is an example of perseverance. He was determined. He stuck to the job. He did things over and over again, even when they were hard, to make sure as many people as possible heard the gospel. In a letter to his friend Timothy, Paul actually said sharing his faith was like a battle: "I have fought a good fight. I have finished the work I was to do. I have kept the faith" (2 Timothy 4:7).

Have there been times when you had to persevere? Times when you could have stopped but chose to keep working at something until you finished the job? That's a good way to please your parents or a boss, and it's a great way to make God happy. When you determine to tell others about His Son, Jesus, He will help you. He'll give you the words you need and the strength to persevere.

Father, help me to persevere even when I feel like stopping.

WRONG WAY, WRONG TIME

Absalom sent men to go in secret through all the families of Israel. He said to them, "As soon as you hear the sound of the horn, then say, 'Absalom is king at Hebron.'"
2 Samuel 15:10

Brave boys do the right thing in the right way at the right time. They don't act like Absalom.

The third son of Israel's King David, Absalom was super good-looking. The Bible says "there was nothing wrong with him from the bottom of his foot to the top of his head" (2 Samuel 14:25). Unfortunately, it seems like Absalom was a little too fond of himself—he thought he should be king.

Absalom didn't care that his dad was already king or that his oldest brother was next for the throne. He got sneaky and tried to steal the kingdom away.

No matter how much we might want something, cheating is never right. If you have a dream, work as hard as you can to make it happen—but don't try to force things that God doesn't allow.

Lord, I want to do the right thing in the right way at the right time. Please guide me in Your path.

DAY 317

FEAR HAS NO REASON TO STAY

There is no fear in love. Perfect love puts fear out of our hearts. People have fear when they are afraid of being punished. The man who is afraid does not have perfect love.
1 JOHN 4:18

We love our friends, and we don't have to be afraid of them. We fear our enemies, but with love, even enemies can become friends.

The Bible says our sin—the wrong stuff that we do—makes us enemies of God. But God can become our friend, and then we don't have to be afraid of Him. Once we accept His love by believing in Jesus, it changes how we think of God.

Many people are afraid of God, since they think He will punish them for doing wrong things. Fearful people don't love very well because fear says, "No one can really love me." But love says, "You are safe, and I will always be here for you."

God's love makes it possible to trust Him. And when you trust His love, fear has no reason to stay.

Lord, help me believe that You love me so much that I don't need to be afraid.

PLANT AND HARVEST

Remember, the man who plants only a few seeds will not have much grain to gather. The man who plants many seeds will have much grain to gather.
2 Corinthians 9:6

Have you ever noticed how the Bible uses picture-stories to explain ideas? The apostle Paul, who wrote this verse, compares the giving of money to planting seeds. When you plant a few seeds, you only get a small crop. But if you plant a lot of seeds, you get a huge crop.

So when it comes to giving money, Paul says, "Plant a lot!" Give away a lot of money so God can use it in big ways. He'll take what you give and turn it into a big crop—a lot of help to people who need it.

But what about me? you might be thinking. *If I give away my money, won't I have needs too?* Yep. And God has that covered. Just a few verses later, Paul said, "God can give you all you need. He will give you more than enough" (2 Corinthians 9:8).

Lord, I want to be a Christian who is known for loving and helping my fellow Christians.

HIS LOVE IS GREATER

"But He knows the way that I take.
When He has tried me, I will come out as gold."
Job 23:10

You remember Job—the faithful man of God who had a whole lot of trouble in his life. The devil kept attacking Job, but God never left his side. God gave Job the strength to go on.

Job reached an important point in his relationship with God—he started to understand that the hard times were going to make him stronger. When we face hard times, it's easy to be sad. Sometimes we feel like we're the only person who has ever had troubles. But that's not true.

Is something in life stressing you out right now? Is something making you worry? Take a minute and ask God to keep you connected to Him. Believe that He is always there, ready to show you the way. Remember that He will use hard times in your life to make you stronger.

Problems can be hard to understand. But always remember that God's love for you is greater than the struggle.

God, please remind me that you are with me, helping me through the hard times.

DAY 320

SHARING WHAT GOD GIVES YOU

"The man who receives much will have to give much. If much is given to a man to take care of, men will expect to get more from him."
LUKE 12:48

In today's verse, Jesus was talking about receiving good things from God. The more you get, the more you should share with others. And Jesus wasn't really talking about shoes, clothes, electronics, sports gear, and other things you own—though you should be willing to share them too. He was actually describing what you *know* about God, the Bible, and the Christian faith. The more you learn, the more you should tell other people.

A guy named Wayne invited one of his school friends to go to church one Sunday. They went again the next week. And on the third Sunday, Wayne's friend heard the good news of the gospel, committed his life to Jesus, and became a Christian.

Do what Wayne did and you'll give a friend the greatest gift ever.

Lord, I never knew sharing the good news was so easy. Help me to do what Wayne did and invite a friend to go to church with me this Sunday.

COMMANDS AND PROMISES

"You have kept Your promise to Your servant, my father David. Yes, You have spoken with Your mouth, and have done it with Your hand, as it is this day."
1 Kings 8:24

Some people think the Bible focuses on the Lord's commands. There certainly are a lot of commands in the Bible, but there are also many wonderful promises. How great that all of God's promises come true!

Imagine the Lord saying, "Hey, I love you! I have designed My promises and commands to bless and enrich you, to guide and protect you." That's not a verse from the Bible, but it's a good summary of what God's words are all about.

That's why you want to spend time each day reading at least one Bible verse. Think about what it means. And then make time to pray. Take God's commands and promises as your guide for each day.

If you've made it this far into this book, you are doing a great job. Keep at it!

Lord, please help me to spend time with You, in Your Word and in prayer. I want to know both Your commands and Your promises!

TEAM CHRISTIAN

I ask you to keep using the gift God gave you.
It came to you when I laid my hands on you
and prayed that God would use you.
2 TIMOTHY 1:6

If you're on a football or robotics or quiz team, you know how important teamwork is. That's true on "Team Christian" too.

Second Timothy is a letter from a wise, older pastor to a younger man learning the ministry. The apostle Paul gave Timothy advice for leading a church but also urged him to be brave and strong. And Timothy could because he had God's gift of leadership. Paul had confirmed that by laying his hands on Timothy's head and praying that God would use him.

Sometimes we think we need to do everything ourselves. We're afraid to ask for advice or help. Don't be like that! God has put older, wiser men in your life to help you grow. Learn from them, follow their example, ask for their prayers.

And someday, before you know it, *you'll* be the older, wiser man. You'll become the coach who keeps Team Christian winning.

Lord, please put wise, older men in my life—and help me to learn from them.

IF, THEN

Dear friends, if God loved us that much,
then we should love each other.
1 John 4:11

Have you noticed how the words *if* and *then* go together? *If* you eat too much candy, *then* you'll get a stomachache. *If* you pull a dog's ears, *then* you'll probably get bitten. Those are examples of *if-then* consequences.

But today's verse shows if and then in a different way. *If* God loves us (and He does), *then* we should love each other. You could say, *Because* God loves us, *then* we should share that love with the people around us.

Some people are easy to love. We smile at them and they smile back. We offer a hand, and they say, "Thank you." But others are harder to love. In fact, some people can be downright mean.

But God loved us while we were still sinners (Romans 5:8), so we should show love to anyone and everyone we meet. It may take some bravery on our parts, but God is happy to help. *If* we pray and ask for courage, *then* He will provide it!

Lord God, I want to follow Your example and share Your love.

LONGING FOR HEAVEN

"After I go and make a place for you, I will come back and take you with Me. Then you may be where I am."
JOHN 14:3

Imagine that you are one of Jesus' original disciples. You've followed Him for a couple years, learning every day. Then one day He says He needs to leave. Don't you think you'd wonder why?

Today's verse provides the reason. Jesus was going away so He could prepare a place for His followers. When He was finished, He'd return to take us all back with Him.

Ever since the crucified and resurrected Jesus rose up into heaven, Christians have longed for His return. And if He didn't return in their lifetime, they knew death would be the door into heaven—a place where God's people never experience tears, pain, or sin. That's something to look forward to!

You're young, so you probably don't think much about dying. But you've probably felt pain and disappointment—a friend has mistreated you or someone you love has died. Hold on to the promise in today's verse. As a believer, you will be with Jesus in heaven someday.

Lord, I can't wait to meet You face-to-face.

REMEMBER GOD ALWAYS

On my bed I remember You. I think of You through the hours of the night.
PSALM 63:6

Your life is really all about God. He made you, and He thinks you're very special. (Reread that last sentence a hundred times if you need to—let its truth sink deep into your mind and heart.) When you understand how important you are to God, you will naturally draw close to Him.

When you feel tired and weak, God is there. He will comfort you in hard times and give you a thousand things to be grateful for. Develop a happy heart by looking around for signs of God's greatness—sunrises and sunsets, mountains and meadows, horses and hawks, friends and family. God's handiwork (and evidence of His love) is all around you.

He loves you with a love that the Bible says is better than anything. So when you go to bed tonight, think about God. He'll be watching over you as you sleep, and He'll lead you into a brave new day tomorrow.

Lord, I thank You for loving me. Even when life is tiring and stressful, I can feel brave knowing that You are in control.

THE BETTER REWARD

You had loving-pity for those who were in prison. . . . For you knew you would have something better in heaven which would last forever.
HEBREWS 10:34

Scientists did an experiment in which kids had to sit at a table with a cookie in front of them. The kids were asked to wait in their spots while the adult stepped out of the room. The kids were told if they waited to eat the cookie, they'd get a second one when the scientist returned. If they didn't want to wait, the kids could just have the one cookie right now.

After this little test, the scientists kept track of those kids for several years. The ones who had waited and got the second cookie were more likely to have good jobs and healthy relationships than the kids who didn't wait.

Can you wait for good things? When we do what God wants, He offers much more than cookies in return. We may not get our rewards immediately, but that just means what we get later will be even better!

Lord, may I do the right thing at the right time, even when I'm not rewarded right away.

BE HONEST

Peter said to Ananias, "Why did you let Satan fill your heart? He made you lie to the Holy Spirit."
Acts 5:3

There's a scary story in Acts 5. A husband and wife dropped dead shortly after they lied about money! Here's how it happened:

After Jesus sent the Holy Spirit to live in believers, the church grew quickly. New Christians gave money to anyone who needed help. They even sold their buildings and land to raise money to help.

One couple, Ananias and Sapphira, sold some of their land. They kept some of the money for themselves but told the church leaders that they were giving it all away. Unfortunately for them, the Holy Spirit told the apostle Peter about their lie. And God made an example of Ananias and Sapphira by taking their lives.

Wow! We can be glad that God doesn't strike *us* dead for the sins we commit today. But the life and death of Ananias and Sapphira show us how seriously God takes lying. The point of this story? Be honest.

Heavenly Father, help me to be truthful when I speak. I know that honesty reflects well on You.

ASKING BOLDLY

"O my God, turn Your ear and hear! Open Your eyes and see our trouble and the city that is called by Your name. We are not asking this of You because we are right or good, but because of Your great loving-pity."
DANIEL 9:18

Daniel was an impressive young guy, maybe only a few years older than you. His country—the Jewish nation of Judah—was attacked and defeated by the army of Babylon. The king of Babylon then rounded up guys like Daniel and took them away to serve in his country. That's where Daniel eventually got in trouble for praying to God. You probably know that he ended up in a den of hungry lions.

Well, God protected Daniel and he came out of the lions' den alive. And he kept praying. One time he admitted to God that he and his people had really messed up. Their disobedience had led to the ruin of their nation!

But Daniel could boldly ask God for forgiveness. Why? Reread today's verse and pay special attention to the last sentence.

Lord God, I want to be brave in prayer, not because I'm good but because You are.

DON'T FREAK OUT

"Peace I leave with you. My peace I give to you.
I do not give peace to you as the world gives.
Do not let your hearts be troubled or afraid."
JOHN 14:27

What do you think *peace* means? You might believe peace is getting along with your friends and never arguing. You might think it's when one nation decides it won't fight another country.

Peace is actually God's gift to you. Jesus left it for you and with you.

Peace is more than just not fighting. God's peace makes you calm even when hard things come into your life. You can be peaceful (as well as joyful, hopeful, and without worry) no matter what's going on around you. You can stay cool because the God of peace will help you.

Believe in God and there's nothing to fear. Don't give your heart permission to freak out. God has the perfect answer for your bad days: peace.

Father, I'm strongest when You help me. You take care of my needs and You tell me I don't have to be troubled or afraid. This isn't easy for me to accept, so please help me.

BRAVE ENOUGH TO CRY

Be sorry for your sins and cry because of them.
Be sad and do not laugh. Let your joy be turned to sorrow.
James 4:9

Many years ago, a boy in Nebraska would open his Bible before bedtime and cry as he read it. Why? Because he was sorry for his sins. Now, as an adult, he still remembers how the pages of that Bible were wet because of his tears.

Have you ever cried over your sins? Different people feel different things, of course, and you won't necessarily cry every time. But if you've never felt the weight of sorrow to the point of shedding tears, then maybe you haven't thought about what your sin cost Jesus. He was perfect—He never did a single thing wrong. Yet He was willing to die a horrible death on the cross for *your* sin—in your place.

Don't try to force tears. Just spend some time today thinking about the high price of your sin. If tears come, that's a good thing.

Father God, I'm so sorry for my sins.
Thank You for sending Jesus to die for them.

SAFE AND SOUND

I am suffering. But I am not ashamed. I know the One in Whom I have put my trust. I am sure He is able to keep safe that which I have trusted to Him until the day He comes again.
2 Timothy 1:12

What if your neighbor had to go away for a while and asked you to take care of her dog? That's an important responsibility. You would work hard to make sure the dog was fed and watered, exercised and protected. If that dog's life was entrusted to you, you'd make sure it was safe and sound when your neighbor returned home.

That's how the apostle Paul said God handles *your* life. In a letter to his friend Timothy, Paul said his own life was hard. He was suffering because so many people hurt him. They arrested him, beat him, and threw him in jail for preaching about Jesus. But he knew that God would protect his soul and spirit. Paul had entrusted himself to God, and God would bring Paul safe and sound into heaven.

He will do the same thing for you.

Father, I put my full trust in You. Keep me safe and sound!

BE A TEACHER

In all things show them how to live by your life and by right teaching.
Titus 2:7

How old do you have to be to teach? If you want to be a schoolteacher, you'd probably be at least twenty-one. But you can actually start teaching right now.

Um, me? No way! Yes, really. *But I don't know how to teach!* Sure you do. *How?* By telling other people what you know. *But I don't know anything!* Of course you do. Just tell what you know is true.

Sometimes, you don't even have to do the talking. You could hand this book to a friend and say, "Hey, read 'Decide Then Follow' on day 184 and tell me what you think." Then wait quietly. Give him a few minutes to consider the words. Keep waiting quietly until he tells you what he thinks. And then still wait quietly. See what he says when he talks a second time. Answer any questions he might have—and if you need to, ask a parent or your pastor for help with any tough questions.

Yes, it's that easy!

Lord, You made sure I read this book. Help me to share its message today.

GOOD SAM

"Then a man from the country of Samaria came by. He went up to the man. As he saw him, he had loving-pity on him. He got down and put oil and wine on the places where he was hurt and put cloth around them. Then the man from Samaria put this man on his own donkey. He took him to a place where people stay for the night and cared for him."

Luke 10:33–34

Most everyone has heard of the Good Samaritan. They know that "Good Samaritans" go out of their way to help others.

The story of the Good Samaritan is a parable—a teaching tool—of Jesus. He told about a Jewish man who'd been attacked by robbers and left for dead. Two other Jewish men, both religious leaders, saw the injured man on the roadside but never stopped to help. Who did? A man from Samaria, a place the Jews hated. The Samaritans weren't fond of the Jews either, but this guy did something brave—he helped, and in a big way.

How did Jesus end His story? By saying, "Go and do the same."

Lord Jesus, show me how to be a "Good Sam"!

SUPERHEROES CAN'T FORGIVE YOU

"But You are a forgiving God. You are kind and loving, slow to anger, and full of loving-kindness."
NEHEMIAH 9:17

Hollywood doesn't make many movies about the one true God, the Creator of heaven and earth. But Hollywood sure makes a lot of movies about superheroes.

Sure, those movies can be exciting to watch. But no superhero could ever do what God does. First, superheroes aren't real. (*Duh.*) Second, even if they *were* real, they wouldn't know you, let alone love you, let alone forgive all your sins. Only God can do that!

God knows you. You already believe that. God loves you. You already believe that too. Jesus died for you to pay the price for your sins. On the third day, Jesus physically rose again from the dead. He's alive now, and He never stops praying for you. He wants you to trust and obey Him all the days of your life.

That's way better than any movie hero.

Lord God, I thank You for what Jesus did for me. I believe the good news. My sins are forgiven! I'm adopted into Your forever family, and You'll never stop loving me.

WORDS THAT GIVE LIFE

Then Jesus said to the twelve followers, "Will you leave Me also?" Simon Peter said to Him, "Lord, who else can we go to? You have words that give life that lasts forever."
JOHN 6:67–68

When Jesus lived on earth, many people came to see Him. They wanted Him to make them well, feed them, or answer their hard questions. In many ways, Jesus was popular.

But there were times when Jesus said things people didn't want to hear. Some of them walked away and never came to see Him again. One time Jesus asked His disciples if they would leave, and Peter had a good answer: "Who else can we go to? You have words that give life that lasts forever."

When you choose to become friends with Jesus, you agree to learn what He likes—and to do what He commands. Even if some of those commands in the Bible are hard or confusing, they are still *God's* commands—and they give life.

Father God, I want to be like Peter. I want to stay close to You and learn the words that give me life—life that lasts forever!

BE SURE OF GOD

Even if an army gathers against me, my heart will not be afraid. Even if war rises against me, I will be sure of You.
Psalm 27:3

Here's a hard thought: We trust a lot of things in this world, but none of them are absolutely certain. Sometimes the brakes fail on the car. Our homes might get knocked down by a hurricane, tornado, or earthquake. Even the people we rely on most can get sick and die.

We can't be sure of anything—except God.

But if we have God, we have everything we need! The writer of this verse, David, knew to trust God in the worst times—even if an army rose up in battle against him. David saw God's power in his life many times. (Remember that knockout of Goliath?) And he trusted that God would show that power again.

God doesn't always take His children out of sticky situations. But He has promised that He will never leave us or give us up (Hebrews 13:5). What do you have to fear when you can be sure of God?

Lord, You are always faithful. Help me to be confident in You.

LOVE = OBEDIENCE

Jesus said, "The one who loves Me will obey My teaching. My Father will love him. We will come to him and live with him."
John 14:23

A man named John the Baptist spent his life telling people about Jesus. He didn't travel the world and put on big shows. He lived a simple life—out in the desert, wearing clothes made of camel hair, eating wild honey and locusts (bugs like grasshoppers). Can you imagine?

One day Jesus came to John, asking to be baptized. John didn't feel like he was good enough to baptize Jesus, but Jesus said that was just the way it should be.

So John obeyed—and then he kept telling people about Jesus. He didn't worry what others thought of him. He didn't waste time wondering how he could become popular. Because John was more interested in Jesus than in himself, God used him to accomplish great things.

And God can use you in the same way. If you love Jesus, obey His teaching. Be like John the Baptist and tell your world about your Lord.

Dear Jesus, please help me to obey Your plan for my life.

DAY 338

FIGHTING AND RUNNING

Fight the good fight of faith.
Take hold of the life that lasts forever.
1 TIMOTHY 6:12

The "good fight of faith" is a strange kind of fight. Most fights have two people circling around each other, looking for chances to land a punch and do some damage.

The fight of faith is more like a race. By His death and resurrection, Jesus already knocked down sin. Now, you can run away while sin is lying on the ground. If you stand there and wait for it to get back up and start swinging again, you are wasting your advantage.

But running away from sin is only part of the fight. What you are running *toward* is just as important as what you are running *from*. God wants you to run toward Him—so focus your eyes on Jesus and go! If you stumble on the way, don't worry. Jesus will step in to protect and help you. You don't have to fight sin alone. Just get back up and start running again. There's safety ahead.

Lord, thanks for fighting for me.
Help me to run away from sin and toward You.

NO GENIES

"If you get your life from Me and My Words live in you, ask whatever you want. It will be done for you."
JOHN 15:7

Have you ever wished you had a genie? That you could rub a lamp, ask for whatever your heart wanted, and get your wish? (You can probably think of a *lot* of things you need or want right now, can't you?)

Christians serve the most powerful being in the universe. We pray to God for things we need. But never think that's like having a genie in a bottle. God gives us many good things but not everything we ask for. Some of them wouldn't be good for us, and others might hurt the people around us. Jesus' promise in today's verse is that God will give us the good things we need when His desires and ours line up. That's what Jesus meant when He said, "If. . .My Words live in you."

This is far better than some imaginary genie in a bottle. We can have a relationship with the one true God through His Son, Jesus—built on prayer.

Father, please make my heart to want what Your heart wants.

TAKING RISKS FOR JESUS

Thomas, who was called the Twin, said to the other followers, "Let us go also so we may die with Jesus."
John 11:16

An eleven-year-old boy named Jeremy sneaked out his bedroom window every Sunday. Why? To go to church.

Jeremy, who lives in the Asian nation of Malaysia, grew up with Muslim parents. The Christian church, he says, was "the only thing that brought me joy." But when his parents realized what he was doing, they sealed his bedroom window to keep him out of church. So Jeremy stayed inside and prayed for his family, hoping they could all come to know Jesus like he did. His actions were risky, and he finally moved in with his grandparents, who accepted his Christian faith.

Following Jesus is more than just obeying rules in the Bible. Sometimes it's about staying faithful to Him in risky situations—even those where you might have to lay down your life.

That takes bravery. But if God calls you to do something, He'll also give you the strength for it. Just let Him live His life through you.

Lord, please quiet my fears as I take risks for You.

GRAB YOUR SWORD!

God's Word is living and powerful. It is sharper than a sword that cuts both ways. It cuts straight into where the soul and spirit meet and it divides them. It cuts into the joints and bones. It tells what the heart is thinking about and what it wants to do.

HEBREWS 4:12

A writer named J. R. R. Tolkien created a fantasy world called Middle Earth. It was filled with creatures like hobbits, elves, dwarves, and talking trees. Two of his hobbit characters, Bilbo and Frodo Baggins, used a special sword named Sting. It would glow blue whenever the ugly, evil orcs were nearby.

In some ways, the Bible is like Sting. It calls itself a sword, and we can use it to defend ourselves from the devil's attacks. And the Bible also warns us of coming trouble. It gets deep into our own thoughts and desires to tell us when we're on the wrong path.

But even better, the Bible shows us the *right* way to go. We can always be bold when we're doing what God's Word says.

Lord, I am protected by Your Word. Help me to handle this "sword" skillfully!

IN TROUBLE

A brother is born to share troubles.
PROVERBS 17:17

If you are a brother, God gave you a big job. Even if you don't have a brother or sister in the home, you have *Christian* brothers and sisters. And you have a big job too.

You get to help when your siblings struggle. You can encourage, support, and pray for them. Even when they haven't been helpful to you. Even when they are rude. Even when you don't want to.

God made family members to help each other. And He wants you to take your job seriously. Your brothers and sisters—at home or at church—might be a pain right now. But as you grow you might just discover that you're there for each other when no one else is. You'll understand each other when no one else can. You will care for each other in the middle of trouble.

It may be hard to believe it now, but God has said, "A brother is born to share troubles."

Father, You say I need to be a brother who is helpful when trouble comes. Make me that kind of brother.

GOOD JOB!

But you, Christian brothers, do not get tired of doing good.
2 THESSALONIANS 3:13

Focus on making good choices. Imagine that each good choice you make is a stone stacked up to build a strong tower of faith. Each one brings you closer and closer to God.

The apostle Paul wrote a letter to Christians in a city called Thessalonica. He wanted them to know that Jesus loved them and was coming back to rescue them from the evil world. But until that day, they should keep living the right way—living for Jesus. Paul told the Thessalonians not to get tired of doing good. He wanted them (and us!) to make being good a habit.

Of course, we'll sometimes make mistakes. But God still loves us. All we need to do is pray and ask Him for forgiveness. Then we can get back on track, building up that habit of doing good. If we do, someday in heaven He'll say to us, "Good job!"

Lord, I really want to be faithful and do what You're calling me to do. Please help me to have a good attitude and not quit when I get tired.

PATIENTLY BRAVE

When people spoke against Him, He never spoke back. When He suffered from what people did to Him, He did not try to pay them back. He left it in the hands of the One Who is always right in judging.

1 Peter 2:23

We know that God's love for us is tender and kind. But what do we do when the situations of our lives are harsh and tough? Well, Jesus is the perfect example of bravery under pressure.

He was about to be horribly killed for "crimes" He never committed. But Jesus knew that that had to happen to give us the chance to be saved from our sin. So He bravely walked toward the cross with love for us as His motivation. And He never complained: "A sheep does not make a sound while its wool is cut. So He made no sound" (Acts 8:32).

Sometimes our own lives will become scary. But, with confidence from Jesus, we can overcome every trouble. Put your trust in Jesus and wait for Him to deliver you.

Dear Jesus, thank You for setting the example of patience and bravery. Help me to live the same way You did!

THE BEST GIFTS

But from your heart you should want the best gifts.
1 Corinthians 12:31

When the Bible says "gifts," it often means *spiritual* gifts—special abilities that God gives to people who accept and follow Jesus. Some spiritual gifts like preaching and teaching put a person in front of others. Those are very important skills, because one person can help dozens, hundreds, or even thousands of other people to understand God's Word and live a better Christian life.

But there can be a danger in gifts like these. When one guy is seen and heard and appreciated by lots of others, pride can creep into his life. That's why the apostle Paul, in his first letter to the Corinthians, urged Christians to want "the best gifts."

What are they? You have to turn the page of your Bible to 1 Corinthians 13 to find the answer: The best gifts are faith, hope, and love. And love is the best of all (1 Corinthians 13:13).

Preaching and teaching aren't for everyone. But anyone can love.

Lord God, please help me to love—
You and the people around me.
I want Your best gifts to make
this world a better place.

READY TO SHARE

Tell them to do good and be rich in good works. They should give much to those in need and be ready to share.

1 Timothy 6:18

Grown-ups often get stressed out paying bills. And some of the biggest, least fun bills are the ones from doctors and hospitals.

A church in West Michigan came up with a plan to help families with their medical bills. Grand Rapids First Church worked with another organization to forgive almost two million dollars' worth of doctor bills for almost nineteen hundred people. They just got a letter in the mail explaining that they no longer needed to pay their bills because the debt had been canceled. How cool is that?

But you don't have to do big, expensive things to change someone's life. If you just share part of your lunch with a student who forgot his or give your jacket to a kid who needs one, they'll remember that kind act for a long, long time. Maybe forever if it causes them to follow Jesus with you!

Lord God, I want to be a Christian who shares much with those in need. Please give me ideas about how to do that.

TIME TO SAY "THANK YOU!"

"For the Son of Man came not to be cared for. He came to care for others."
MATTHEW 20:28

Think about someone who's rich, famous, and powerful. What do they do all day? Do you think they do all the work? Absolutely not. They tell *other* people what to do. It's work, work, work for everyone but the top dog.

Except when it comes to the Lord God, Creator of heaven and earth. When God sent His Son to earth, Jesus didn't zoom in on a helicopter and start bossing people around. Just the opposite! Jesus said He came to *care* for other people. And not just a little bit. He showed the world what God is really like by dying on the cross for our sins.

It's amazing to realize that God loves you so much. He sent Jesus to rescue you, forgive all your wrongdoing, adopt you into His forever family, and give you a brand-new life. There's more, but you get the idea. It's time to say, "Thank You!"

Lord, You sent Your Son, Jesus, to serve me both now and forever. Thank You, indeed!

NO FEAR IN OBEDIENCE

Say to those whose heart is afraid, "Have strength of heart, and do not be afraid. See, your God will come ready to punish. He will come to make sinners pay for their sins, but He will save you."
ISAIAH 35:4

Does it seem that different people play by different rules? Your mom or dad tells you to respect others, but no one else seems to do that. You're told to be kind, but many people are rude. You're asked to love others, but some people you know just seem to spread hate.

In the Bible, God gave the rules that He wants people to follow. Some people ignore the rules, and others just refuse to follow them.

Isaiah was one of God's messengers called "prophets." He saw many people making excuses for ignoring God's rules. Isaiah knew that those people would face consequences for their disobedience. Someday God will make them pay.

But if you want to obey God, Isaiah had good news: You can be strong, knowing that you will be saved. There is no fear in obedience.

Father, obeying You means I'm willing to follow You in the greatest adventures of life.

SHADOW OF WINGS

My soul goes to You to be safe. And I will be safe in the shadow of Your wings until the trouble has passed.
Psalm 57:1

God loves you and shows you kindness in so many ways. This truth should help you trust Him no matter what's happening. God will always lead you in the right way. Your job is to spend time with Him, reading His Word and praying and "listening" for what He tells you to do.

Psalm 57 was written by David, who was running for his life from the jealous King Saul. Even when he was hiding in a cave, David called to God for help. His enemies were trying to distract him, but David kept his attention on the Lord.

How can you keep your focus on God? Think about the times of your day when you worry or wonder. Turn those into Bible reading and prayer times! Trust God to help you overcome your fears. He promises to keep you safe, like a baby bird under the protective wings of its mother.

Lord God, I thank You for keeping me safe from the troubles of this world. May I always keep my focus on You.

HOLDING GOD'S HAND

Keep a strong hold on your faith in Christ. May your heart always say you are right. Some people have not listened to what their hearts say. They have done what they knew was wrong. Because of this, their faith in Christ was wrecked.

1 Timothy 1:19

Holding on to your faith is a bit like a toddler holding his father's hand. The father's grip is stronger than the toddler's, but each one is holding the other's hand. It's the same way with faith. God is stronger, and He isn't going to let you go. But things will go easier when you aren't trying to pull Him somewhere He doesn't intend to go.

God has mapped out the perfect life for you. He wants to keep you close and guide you. When you do something you know is wrong, it's like you're trying to pull God off the path. That will only lead to hurt.

Keep holding God's hand. Do the things you know are right. Stay on the path. Your journey isn't as much about where you're headed as it is about whose hand you hold.

Lord, keep my grip strong as I hold Your hand.

NOT SILENT

Teach all these things and give words of help. Show them if they are wrong. You have the right and the power to do this. Do not let anyone think little of you.

Titus 2:15

We don't know exactly how old Titus was. But he may have been a younger man. When you read the apostle Paul's words in today's verse, you get the feeling that Titus knew how it felt to be treated like a little kid. Have you ever gone through that yourself?

Paul had left Titus on the island of Crete in the Mediterranean Sea to find leaders for the church there. Apparently, a lot of people did not want to listen to what Titus had to say. So Paul told Titus to stand up for himself as he shared the truth of the gospel. Titus shouldn't let people's rude reactions get in the way of the message of Jesus.

It's frustrating when you feel like no one is listening. But, like Titus, don't let that stop you. Continue to speak the truth in love.

Father, sometimes I feel intimidated. Please help me to speak up and share my faith.

WEARING A MASK

Even while laughing the heart may be in pain,
and the end of joy may be sorrow.
PROVERBS 14:13

A great preacher named John Wesley once said, "The outward signs of joy are often mixed with real sorrow." Have you ever seen that to be true? Maybe you were sad to attend a funeral, but you still laughed at a funny story somebody told about the person who had passed away.

Since people in pain don't always show it, keep an eye out for little signals in those you love. If they're hurting, you can walk through their pain with them. If you do notice sadness, it may take courage on your part to say something. But if you speak in a loving manner, the person you are trying to help will appreciate it.

On the other hand, if *you're* the one covering up pain with laughter, be brave enough to tell someone that you need support—even if they didn't spot it right away. The Christian life is all about helping each other.

Lord, Galatians 6:2 says to "help each other in troubles and problems." Give me the courage to do that.

GO AHEAD AND ASK

Jesus said to him, "What do you want Me to do for you?" The blind man said to Him, "Lord, I want to see!"
MARK 10:51

"Blind Bart" sat at the roadside, begging for money. Everyone entering or leaving Jericho saw him there, day after day, scraping up money to live on.

One day, when he learned the miracle-working Jesus was nearby, Bart (full name: Bartimaeus) started shouting: "Son of David, take pity on me" (Mark 10:48). Jesus heard Bart, stopped, and called him over. Then Jesus asked what he wanted.

"Oh, nothing," Bart answered. "I just thought I'd say hi."

Um, no. Blind Bart was quick to answer, "Lord, I want to see!"

If you're a follower of Jesus, God *wants* you to ask for things—your daily food, forgiveness of your sins, protection from temptation. You can also ask for your friends to know Jesus, wisdom in decision-making, even—like Bart—healing for yourself and others.

Sometimes God will say no to your requests, but until He does, go ahead and ask. He might very well say yes!

Lord God, I want to see everything You have for me in Your Word.

FRIENDS

"No one can have greater love than to give his life for his friends."
JOHN 15:13

Jesus calls you a friend, and you have to like the sound of that. Being a friend of Jesus means He loves you and wants to spend time with you. You can trust Him because He proved His love for you. He died on the cross to pay the price for your sin.

Since He is God, Jesus was the only one who *could* pay for your sin. And He did that willingly. That's great news!

But there's even better news: Three days later, Jesus rose from the dead to prove His power over death. When He says He can give you eternal life, He knows what He's saying.

Jesus laid down His life for you so you could really live as a child of God. He loves you. He's your truest friend. That should make you brave.

Father God, I like having friends I can trust. I like having friends who are close. Thank You for sending Jesus as proof of Your love, to be the closest, most trustworthy Friend I can ever have.

GLAD IN GOD

May the words of my heart be pleasing to Him.
As for me, I will be glad in the Lord.
PSALM 104:34

Do you ever wonder how big God is? You should—because the bigger He is to you, the more you will enjoy Him. He is the wonderful Creator who made you. He sets the rules and guides you in the way you should go. He is great and glorious, wise and loving.

Everything we see reflects God's mighty design. He takes care of the land and the animals. He guards the trees and guides the rivers. Nothing is an accident! A time may come when you wonder about your purpose in the world. Don't fret—God is always leading and protecting you.

Because of that, you can keep a positive perspective even when life seems crazy. Let your life be a song that you sing to God in thanksgiving. Let your thoughts and actions be the worship you lift up to Him in praise.

Lord God, I want to stay positive. Some days that's hard to do, so please show me how to be faithful despite my circumstances. I want to be glad in You!

GOD DOESN'T LIE

"God is not a man, that He should lie. He is not a son of man, that He should be sorry for what He has said. Has He said, and will He not do it? Has He spoken, and will He not keep His Word?"
NUMBERS 23:19

From cover to cover, the Bible makes it crystal clear that *God doesn't lie*. The Bible is also clear that the devil, also known as Satan, *always* lies. Jesus even called him "the father of lies" (John 8:44). If Satan ever says anything true, it's only so he can mix that truth with untruths.

So how can you guard against the devil's deceptions? Well, you have to really know God's truth! The more you read and study the Bible, the better you'll be at spotting Satan's lies.

Here's an example: Satan says that you have to be really, really good to please God. But the Bible says God is pleased when you believe in the work of His really, really good Son, Jesus. Then when you become a follower of Jesus, God helps you to *become* really, really good.

No lie!

Lord, please protect me from Satan's half-truths and lies.

CAN'T MICROWAVE THIS

The Lord is good to those who wait for Him, to the one who looks for Him.
LAMENTATIONS 3:25

Microwave ovens are great. You stick a bag of popcorn inside and get a hot, fresh snack in a couple of minutes. A bowl of ravioli could take even less time.

But microwave ovens can make us think *everything* should go fast. And that's not how life works—especially not the Christian life. Many times God wants us to slow down, to be patient, to wait for Him to move in our lives. If we expect microwave results, we'll be frustrated. We won't please God and we won't help anyone else.

That's why brave boys live out the message of Lamentations 3:25. They know that God is good to the guys who wait for Him. They know that God blesses boys who patiently watch for Him.

How do we do that? We get to know Him through His Word. We pray as often as we can. Every time we stop to remind ourselves that God is there (and in control), we gain His goodness in our lives.

Lord, life is not a microwave oven. Please help me to be patient!

BEING LIKE CHRIST

Dear friends, we are God's children now. But it has not yet been shown to us what we are going to be. We know that when He comes again, we will be like Him because we will see Him as He is.

1 John 3:2

We don't know everything about what life will be like in heaven, but scripture does give us hints. Today's verse says we will be "like Him." In what way? Albert Barnes, an old-time Bible teacher, believed we would be like Him not just in our new, everlasting bodies, but "in character, in happiness, in glory." What does that mean?

Think about it: Your character will be perfected—you won't even want to lie or cheat or steal. You'll have a heavenly happiness—not in the short term but for all eternity—so you won't ever feel sad again. And the work that Jesus has done in you will be for God's glory, meaning He gets all the credit.

What could be better than that?

Father God, I can't wait to be made just like Jesus. But until that time in eternity, please make me more like Him every day on earth.

GIFTS THAT PLEASE GOD

Remember to do good and help each other. Gifts like this please God.
Hebrews 13:16

Andy and his brother loved Gil, an older man in their church. And Gil loved everybody. At Christmastime, he would buy dozens of stuffed animals to give to the little kids at church. When Gil came down with cancer and died, Andy and his brother were sad. But then they got an idea.

The boys collected all of their old stuffed animals. They put all fifty-two of them into big white plastic bags. The next Sunday, Andy and his brother gave the bags to Gil's wife, asking her, "Would you please give these away to the littler kids?" She was surprised but happy to say yes.

These boys were living out the truth of Hebrews 13:16: They remembered to do good. They helped other people. And the gifts they gave pleased God.

Is there anything similar you could do?

Lord, I could give away the stuff I don't play with anymore and make some younger kids—and You—happy. Please help me to follow through like Andy and his brother did.

WHO'S DRIVING?

Jesus said to His followers, "If anyone wants to be My follower, he must forget about himself. He must take up his cross and follow Me."
MATTHEW 16:24

Imagine you're a car. Go ahead, pick your favorite. It's probably a nice one, right? So, who will you let drive you? After all, you're a sharp, expensive vehicle.

Would you let your twelve-year-old friend drive? How about a stranger? Probably not. You might not trust them to be as careful as they should be. They might drive too fast, hit a guardrail (maybe even a pedestrian), or never bring you back to the garage. Whew, it's dangerous to be a hot car!

Of course, you're *not* a car. But you still have to be careful who drives (you could say "influences") your life. Many people will tell you the wrong things and point you in the wrong direction. But not Jesus.

Do what He says in the Bible, and you'll never go wrong. When Jesus "drives" you, He'll never scratch your paint or dent your fender. He'll steer you straight into the perfection of heaven.

Lord, make me wise enough to know that I should always follow where You lead.

FIRE OF SUFFERING

"See, I have tested you, but not as silver.
I have tested you in the fire of suffering."
ISAIAH 48:10

Life is full of hard things. Sometimes we get sick. Sometimes we face bullies. Sometimes parents divorce. Sometimes. . .well, fill in your own "hard thing" here.

Many tough things happen just because our world is broken. Sin makes people selfish, and their actions affect us even when we haven't done anything wrong. But once in a while, our *own* sin creates trouble for us. There are times when God allows suffering to catch our attention and draw us back to Himself.

That's what God did with the people of Israel. He used prophets like Isaiah to warn the people, to remind them of His rules, to try to get them to turn from sin and back to God. But when they didn't listen, He sent the "fire of suffering."

We can't avoid every problem in this broken world. But we don't have to *ask* for trouble by disobeying God! If you know what He wants you to do, just do it.

Lord God, please help me to obey You the first time, every time.

WORD AND DEED

"Is it not a time to share your food with the hungry, and bring the poor man into your house who has no home of his own? Is it not a time to give clothes to the person you see who has no clothes?"
Isaiah 58:7

It's one thing to tell God you want to follow Him. It is another thing to do what He wants. If your good intentions only go as far as your words, then your commitment to God is less than He deserves.

If you are ready to show God you love Him, start by loving the people made in His image. How can you tell who was made in God's image? Simple: *Every* person was made in the image of God! Everyone bears the mark of God's creation and should be treated with love and respect.

God wants you to do the right thing for the right reason. Show love to others, not because of what they look like or how much money they have but because of who made them. Follow God in word and deed.

Lord, may my actions match my words when I say that I love You.

MAKE IT RIGHT

"Do not lie about the weight or price of anything. Always tell the truth about it."
Leviticus 19:35–36

You remember Zaccheus? He collected taxes from his fellow Jews and gave the money to the Roman government. That was bad enough, but he also lied, saying people owed more than they really did. He grew rich by cheating.

Zaccheus and his other tax-collector friends were called "sinners" by other people who hated their dishonesty. But one day Jesus asked to visit Zaccheus's house for dinner. Can you believe that? Zaccheus couldn't either. While Jesus ate with him, Zaccheus had a major change of heart.

"Lord, see!" he said. "Half of what I own I will give to poor people. And if I have taken money from anyone in a wrong way, I will pay him back four times as much" (Luke 19:8). Jesus said that promise proved that Zaccheus had truly been saved.

It's always best to be honest. But even if you've done something wrong, be like Zaccheus. Admit it, and make it right.

Heavenly Father, please help me to be honest in all that I do.

CALL ON THE LORD TODAY

"Look for the Lord while He may be found.
Call upon Him while He is near."
ISAIAH 55:6

When you're young, it seems like you have all the time in the world. A whole year—from birthday to birthday or Christmas to Christmas—feels like forever. But if you're twelve or ten or even eight right now, you can remember a lot of years that have already passed. Someday you'll wake up and realize that you're an adult, that life has actually flown by. It happens to everyone.

And that's why we have verses like Isaiah 55:6 above. If life is like fog ("you see it and soon it is gone," James 4:14 says), then *right now* is the time to "look for the Lord." *Right now* is the time to "call upon Him." God is just waiting for you to say, "Yes, Lord—I believe in You, I trust in You, I want Jesus Christ to be my Savior."

Have you made that call yet? God is on the other end, just waiting to answer.

Father in heaven, I want to be part of Your family. I call on You today for salvation through Jesus Christ.

YOUR JOB

Keep yourselves in the love of God. Wait for life that lasts forever through the loving-kindness of our Lord Jesus Christ.
Jude 21

God loved us before we ever loved Him (1 John 4:19). God showed that love by sending Jesus to die for us when we were still sinners (Romans 5:8). And He "chose us for Himself because of His love" (Ephesians 1:4).

Christians join God's family only because He made the choice to love us first. But now we have a job—to *keep* ourselves in His love. How do we do that?

Jesus said, "If you love Me, you will do what I say" (John 14:15). We obey what He's told us to do in His Word. When we do that, we "abide" in Him—that's an old-fashioned word that means we "live in" Jesus. Or, as He said in John 15:5, "Get your life from Me." We are just branches who must be connected to Jesus, the vine.

If we stay connected to Jesus, there's nothing to fear. He will see us through this life and into eternity with Him!

Lord, please help me to do my job—to keep myself in Your love.

SCRIPTURE INDEX

OLD TESTAMENT

Micah

Zechariah

Malachi

NEW TESTAMENT

Matthew

Mark

Luke

***One Devotion a Day for Boys* entries were written by**

Bob Evenhouse: Days 5, 13, 23, 33, 43, 49, 55, 67, 78, 85, 96, 106, 118, 126, 132, 138, 150, 162, 171, 181, 189, 200, 209, 220, 232, 244, 268, 280, 292, 304, 315, 327, 339, 351, 363

David Sanford: Days 7, 10, 19, 21, 31, 35, 37, 47, 59, 61, 70, 73, 79, 82, 91, 97, 102, 108, 114, 121, 130, 139, 144, 151, 157, 163, 164, 169, 176, 183, 195, 196, 201, 208, 213, 221, 225, 234, 237, 246, 249, 259, 262, 272, 284, 286, 290, 296, 298, 308, 320, 321, 332, 334, 347, 356, 359

Glenn Hascall: Days 2, 8, 14, 20, 26, 32, 38, 44, 50, 56, 62, 68, 74, 80, 86, 92, 98, 104, 110, 116, 122, 128, 134, 141, 146, 153, 159, 166, 172, 178, 184, 191, 197, 204, 210, 216, 222, 227, 233, 239, 245, 251, 257, 263, 269, 275, 281, 287, 293, 299, 305, 311, 317, 329, 335, 342, 348, 354, 360

Josh Mosey: Days 4, 17, 29, 41, 52, 64, 77, 88, 100, 112, 124, 136, 147, 158, 170, 182, 194, 207, 219, 231, 243, 255, 267, 279, 302, 314, 326, 338, 350, 362

Lee Warren: Days 3, 9, 16, 22, 34, 39, 45, 51, 57, 69, 75, 81, 87, 93, 99, 105, 111, 117, 123, 129, 135, 142, 148 ,154, 160, 167, 173, 179, 185, 192, 198, 211, 217, 223, 229, 235, 241, 247, 252, 258, 264, 270, 276, 282, 288, 294, 300, 306, 312, 318, 324, 330, 336, 340, 346, 352, 358

Matt Koceich: Days 6, 12, 24, 30, 36, 42, 48, 54, 66, 72, 76, 84, 89, 95, 101, 107, 113, 125, 131, 137, 143, 155, 161, 168, 174, 180, 186, 193, 199, 212, 218, 224, 230, 236, 242, 248, 254, 260, 265, 271, 277, 283, 289, 295, 301, 307, 313, 319, 325, 331, 337, 343, 349, 355, 361

Paul Kent: Days 1, 15, 18, 27, 28, 40, 53, 60, 63, 65, 90, 94, 103, 109, 115, 119, 127, 133, 140, 145, 149, 152, 165, 175, 177, 187, 188, 190, 202, 203, 205, 206, 214, 215, 226, 228, 238, 240, 250, 253, 256, 261, 266, 273, 274, 278, 285, 291, 297, 303, 310, 316, 322, 323, 328, 333, 341, 345, 353, 357, 364, 365

Zech Haynes: Days 11, 25, 46, 58, 71, 83, 120, 156, 309, 344